LEEDS & SELECTED WRITINGS

Also by *Barry Tebb*

Poetry

Five Quiet Shouters (Peter Redgrove, Wendy Oliver, Michael Holmes, John Cotton, Angela Carter) – editor 1966

The Quarrel with Ourselves 1966

Three Regional Voices (with Iain Crichton Smith & Michael Longley 1968)

Crosscurrents 1970

The Lights of Leeds 2001

Tranquillity Street 2004

Selected Poems 1964 – 2004

Sixties Press Anthology of Gregory Fellows' Poetry (editor with Debjani Chatterjee) 2004

The Real Survivors Anthology 2006

The Nostalgia Bus – Collected Poems 2007

Orphans of Albion (with Survivors Press) 2008

The Leeds Poetry Renaissance 2012

Mental Health

Kith and Kin – Experiences in Mental Health Caring 2004

Beyond Stigma – Experiences of Mental Health Survivors 2006

The Overdose 2007

Schreber Revisited 2007

Young Carers Handbook 2008

Other

The Fiddler and his Bow (Autobiography) 2005

Pitfall Street (Novel) 2005

Acid Drops – Collected Reviews 2005

Strangers on the Shore: Tales of Immigrant Life 2008

Leeds
&
Selected Writings

of

Barry Tebb

Goldfish Press, Seattle

Published by Goldfish Press, an imprint of Chrysanthemum Publications, Inc.

ISBN 13: 978-1-950276-28-8
ISBN 10: 1-950276-27-9
Library of Congress Control Number 2024933646

Book Design: Russel Davis
Cover Photo: Peter Astbury Under Creative Commons License

Goldfish Press is a literary press of all genres.
Goldfish Press
4545 42nd Ave SW
Suite 211
Seattle, WA 98116-4243

Website: poetrychrysanthemum.com

Preface

I was born in a back-to-back in Leeds in 1942. Our house was in the heart of South Leeds, literally a stone's throw from the suspension bridge over the Aire that was to be a central symbol in my poems and novellas.

The working-class life I enjoyed was quite wonderful. It wasn't of course a life of council estates, drug-gangs and ghetto-blasters. It was essentially a sense of community, of shared values and even – in hard times – shared food. Above all it provided a sense of being cared for and protected, not just by my parents but by neighbours and other children.

Among these children was Margaret Gardiner ('Margaret Hopwood' in my novellas). It is nearly half a century since I last saw her but she was the very first person to encourage me to write stories and she was my first audience sitting on the hot July pavements of our enchanted summers. She also taught me the dialect of working class Leeds and she was my first love. After twenty five years of not being able to write (1970–1995) it was a deep and powerful dream of her that started off my writing again. In the dream she appeared against a background of the Aire and the suspension bridge saying, – "I am here, I am waiting."

Silver water lapped in the dream river, multiple rainbows arced in the air and diamonds danced as together we skipped down the steps to the towpath. The 'working through', as Freud would have called it, of the manifest and latent dream content provided the material for nearly all my recent poems, especially the long autobiographical poem, 'The Bridge Over the Aire' and my first two novellas, *Margaret* and *Margaret Gone.*

I have walked and walked round the few bits of my childhood Leeds that remain, especially along the banks of the Aire and in Kirkgate Market, that living museum of the folk memory.

When I was twelve my family moved to a council estate on the edge of the city and at the same time I attended a horrendously repressive all boys grammar school. When I was sixteen we moved again, this time to the mill village of Yeadon between Bradford and Leeds, and it was at this time, sitting watching the glide of the swans on the Tarn, that I wrote my first poems. I began to read modern poetry, especially James Kirkup ('My James Kirkup', my contribution to *Diversions,* Salzburg University Press. 1998, a collection for the poet's eightieth birthday), Auden, Dylan Thomas and Thomas Blackburn, to name only a few.

After a year's unqualified teaching I went to Leeds Teacher Training College. It was the sixties and the atmosphere of the college was very liberal and one in which I flourished. I read widely, Proust, Firbank, Dickens, Ginsberg, Sartre, Kierkegaard, and 'The New Poetry' (Plath, Lowell and Berryman). My poems and articles started to appear in magazines such as *Peace News* and *The Poetry Review* and Alan Tarling (of Poet & Printer Press) brought out my first collection, *The Quarrel With Ourselves,* which was fortunate to get a good review in The New Statesman from John Carey, now Merton Professor of English at Oxford and a future Booker Prize judge. This was the period of the Gregory Fellows in Poetry at Leeds University (why are there no more?) such as John Silkin, David Wright, Peter Redgrove, and most importantly, the wonderful Martin Bell.

I tried my hand at editing a small anthology of contemporary poets and included Redgrove, Angela Carter - who was a poet before she was a novelist, John Cotton, Michael Holmes, and Wendy Oliver (she was a first-class poet, I wonder what happened to her!) Tarling also brought out a 'three poets from three regions' anthology, Michael Longley represented Northern Ireland, Iain Crichton Smith, Scotland, and myself the North of England. Although the book appeared in the sixties, Tarling said he was receiving orders for it - though it was long out of print – until his press closed in 1996. When I finished at college I went to teach at Wyther Park School, Leeds Five, the title/subject of a recent poem published in *Poetry and Audience*, a magazine which had published my work thirty years before. I was very fortunate in being given an 'A' stream of ten year olds, and I taught almost nothing but poetry and painting from nine until four.

My experiences in getting children to write were recorded in an article for Peace News, 'Poetry in the Classroom'. The climax of this period was having my poem 'School Smell' included in the ground-breaking Penguin anthology, *Children of Albion* in 1969, alongside poets like Roy Fisher, Jim Burns, Lee Harwood, Adrian Mitchell, Edwin Morgan, Tom Pickard and Andrew Crozier. It sold more than a hundred thousand copies in a very short time, some indication of how hot poetry was in the Sixties!

—Barry Tebb

Contents

The Quarrel With Ourselves (1966)

from Three Regional Voices (1968)

Crosscurrents (1970)

The Lights of Leeds (2001)

Tranquillity Street (2004)

from **The Nostalgia Bus(2007)**

Uncollected

Translations, *Poems from the French* (2007)

In Memoriam

Leeds
&
Selected Writings

The Quarrel With Ourselves
(1966)

School Smell

Composed of chalk dust,
Pencil shavings and
The sharp odour
Of stale urine;

It meets me now and then
Creeping down a creosoted corridor
Or waiting to be banged
With the dust from piles of books
On top of a cupboard.
The double desks heeled with iron
Having long been replaced;
The steel-nibbed pens and
Ink watered to pale grey
Gone too: the cane's bamboo bite
Has nothing left to bite on
And David's psalms
Must learn each other.

But it's there
Ready to spring out
Like a coiled snake skin still envenomed
After years by a suburban hearth.

It was fifteen years ago
But I still remember Smigger,
Our greying old headmaster
In his spats and striped trousers,
The last in our town to wear them,
And his northern accent,
Heavy as Sunday.

"Now then you lads,
I'm not having this
Or I'll tan you all,"
He'd bawl at a mill-hand's boy
For drawing cunts on the lavatory wall.

Old Holmes, too, his yellow teeth
And hair all over the place,
One hand trembling with shell shock.

The other with rage, one foot lame
And brain half daft,
Ready to belt you
For moving an eye.

The boys were always
Belching and farting
And tormenting me for my
Long words and soft voice
And they do still
When I sense that stink
In my nostrils.

Change

As milled silver I was welcome
In every gutter, tinkling over cobbles
I rang the truth loudly on solid-oak counters
And tills tolled for me clear as bells.

Boldly I gave myself to many,
Slipped from moist palm to pocket,

Pirouetting without points, jingling
With dull coppers and important keys.

First I was lost in a hundred
Children's essays, found myself
With pearls in secret pockets,
Counterfeit and shiny.
Then I discovered in a deed-box,
Frowned over as I beamed a dusty smile
Of centuries, polished till I pierced the fondness
Nastily, with a sickly yellow glare.
My smooth face made the end easy;
I piled up with the rest, counted and
Columned, exchanging memories
In a sudden hot flood of death.

Disorderly Conduct

The poet, alone at snowfall,
Must be insane
To feel the cold
Hand of God.
Neurotic, of course, to consider
His breathing might shatter
The flakes' fluid pattern
Frosting the glass.

Hurrying from the house
To be caught disturbing
The orderly procession of weathers
His disorderly mind endeavours
To unify the falling fragments
And make lucid the chaos
Of his mind's kingdom.

If the Zulu believe rain
Is a god weeping
For dead birds,
Our easy acceptance
Of its frozen flood -
At worst a background for comic cards,
At best a poet's trope -
Rainbows no starry promise
For the spirit's darker skies.

Miro's The Rays of the Sun Wound the Lingering Star

A child could gather
Every part in a morning's
Play and similarly spiral
Stars across a canvas.

A child's pillow could hold
The grimacing golliwog
Cloaked in a rainbow
That is the artist's dream.
The acid sophistication
Of his scrawl
Enacts a clockwork
Nightmare.

In a toy universe
The red moon leers,
Illuminates the mad
Airscape's moment.

Only the necklace
Of black sunspot's
Clustering could not
Be a child's.

Vincent van Gogh

He never knew whether
He was mad or sane;
'Truly you paint like a madman',
Cezanne, the master, said,
Raw red streaks on the canvas,
Blood from a severed ear,
Unable to understand the worldliness
Of Gauguin yet respecting his art,
Even trying to be a Christian,
Selling his goods,
But not his pictures.
Taking a street woman off the streets
To save her, was cursed for it:
'You are a vicious character',
An art dealer said.
Gauguin, whom he tried to help.
Could not stand his naivete
Ironically declared, 'Corporal
You are right', then fled
From the provincial's hurt-
'I wish I could die now',
Were his last words, the works
Scattered round his tousled bed,
Still misunderstood, and said,
In a last letter to a friend.
'What's the use?'

A Kind of Distraction

You always disrupt me;
When I ring you for comfort
You wing me, send my
Pudding of a mind
A splatter on the wall.

You chase me to bed even,
Passionately, not-yourself-at-all,
You bawl your lewd reminders
Down aching avenues of dreams
To shudder me awake.
And then at last you'll fake
Your promises and take
Some simpler way, battening
On the eggs you'll hatch
Warmly some tea-cosy day.

All this, you'll say, was
Merely adolescence, not
The real unpoked you,
Tittupping in high heels
And cellophaned to view.

The Children

Autumn to them means
Most of all leaves
Twirling russet skeletons
Underfoot for crunching,
Boughs spangled silver-grey
Or red with squirrels on them.
(Really their unbecoming bark
Crawls with damp white fungi,
Less than half have seen
A squirrel and I cannot disturb
One's innocent vision of 'squirrel'
On the canal bank, the slinking
Rat among weeds and corpses).
Conkers, gathering scars, do battle
Out of uniform, stars crisp the night,
Sparrows squatting on the ledge
Edge between me and the rain
And the children, whose view
Remains musical. Autumn is still
Encrusting the rain-spattered
Window, demanding admission,
Dissolving the flesh of innocence.

For an Infants' Poem Book

Faded Father Christmases in pillar-box red
And cotton-wool beards, hanging bags bulging
Number cards where a million dots dancing like weirds
Tiered the wall: I remember it all now, Mrs Burns
Wrapped in ratskin talked to herself about God -
And chewed the dangling stumps of her teeth,
Starched Miss Smith barked and brayed in tweedy green,
Made me count beads on a bead frame from nine to four.

And always in the playground rotting apple cores,
Orange skins bleached like bones in the sun,
Weeds springing in crevices as I run
From the terrifying cries of the children
Falling like blows.

Ibsen at Seventy

The room exhales its odours,
Musk rose and powdered lavender
Haunt his nostrils, one side of him
Breathes awareness of them.
He is trying to write something,
His name; the pen refuses him,
Ink dries out his mind.
His head is made of blotting paper,
It is saturated with the names
Of his children, but he forgets
Why he made them.
All he remembers is that fame
Once dripped like honey
From the hives of his mind;
Now his memory runs like water.
His tongue crackles thirstily;
He is crying like a child.

Expectancy

Lodged in some deep recess of the soul
Poems are waiting for me to write them;
They are growing in me like a cancer ,
Each one a nub of pain, weaving untidily
Between the unsound organs of sense.

Whenever I breathe I exhale the odd
Unwritten, unspoken as yet even unthought
Half-line. What swells between stomach and head
May be the stanza I thought was lost, exploring
The labyrinthine coils of blood and gut.

The deft movement of my hand on paper (stabler
Than the shaking inner wrist of doubt) makes
Me wonder who or what guides the pen, makes me
Tremble at what I may unwittingly leave out.
Re-write? I can hardly make a fair copy...

And yet they come; maybe trailing along,
An urchin gang sobbing and snotty-nosed,
But getting somewhere, however late, arriving
Unnoticed on the dusty blank page
Of an unread book none bothers to cast out.

Morning Walk

for Barbara

I step off the pavement like a precipice
Engage the darting sunshafts in a duel
In the wall's shadow I web my prints to pattern
The moist stone virgins.

The lawns are white-coated their throats red
With berries and bird-song; in petrified gardens
Hyacinth tongues lip the wall.

Leaf mould muffles my heel-taps the enormous trees
Totter in the hyaline air; I hear the Sunday strollers in their
Mist-making walks, pressing through them
Like some voiceless ghost.

The Quarrel with Ourselves

Baronial junketings
Flash red and purple vestments
Shields clash and swords
But the essential blazonings
Are in the heart.

Platonic dialogues were really
Solo performances - from the wall's shelter
To the underlying form lay an intricate
Network of pathways - crossroads
Within a single mind.
The rampant lion netted by the mouse
Produced only a temporary liaison -
Each fable's cardboard house
An analogue for externals only, the central truth
The quarrel with ourselves.

from Three Regional Voices
(*with Michael Longley and Iain Crichton Smith*)
(1968)

Everything in its Place

Desks are straining on all fours, flanks
Heaving to hurl the hunched riders
Down crack and cranny, buck
Finger-snapping lids, consume
Scrap and scribble between tongue and teeth.

The blackboard is cleaning itself behind me,
Making my neck prick as it scatters dust
Like seed, empties its clogged pores of cliché,
Anoints its carved channels and cavities
With infinite black ooze and sap.

And I don't trust that corner cupboard!
Opening its dark doors like the jaws of
Cerberus, shelving its stacks to heave
At my head, ready to snap its quick lock
Round my wrist like a crab.

I watch the windows wink and blink,
Tug at their catches, tempt my fingers
With their openings, crack flying cords
To noose my neck; they eye the bulging roof
Beams, bent like a bow above me.

This whole room has rushed to the world's edge,
My fingers tip its tottering walls
Braced to hold definition, floorboards
Knotted tight against infinity's axe, doors
Bolted to contain time and place in time and place together.

I cry 'help' as my world whirls,
Is loosed at the single eye of heaven.

Gauguin in the South Seas

They have my own fear of the dark,
Tupapau – spirits of the dead they call it;
Returning late with oil I found fear of it
Had spread my vahine naked on the bed.

Manao-Taipapau means 'she thinks of the spectre'
Or 'the spectre is thinking of her', either way
She is afraid; I marvel at a tongue so readily ambiguous,
Lying across her forked thigh.

I buy rum for her 'many parents', for her
One cheap dress a month suffices; in return
She gathers fish and wild-fruit from the blue
Mountain groves where no white man walks.
Once when I fished from the long canoes
A fish caught the hook in its lower jaw, laughing
I learnt this meant my vahine was unfaithful:
She answered 'Beat me' but I lay down by her side.

I bathe in 'the stream of life', naked to offend
The priestly beetles - Cezanne's 'red shout' indeed.
Waiting for mail I accumulate bills, pictures and sores
Side by side, lying down alone in the dark.

For Two Friends

1

***for* Larry**

Pushing memory
From me to you
Like darkness
From a lighted train
However hard you look
Your eyes will strain
The darkness pull
Memory from the mirror
Push it back again.
Blotting 'Now' with 'Then'
I mutter 'How?' I
Am not free:
You hold the moving room,
Draw in the things and me.

2

***for* Wendy**

Poetry , 'the stuff' so dearly wrought
A blood count of the lines
Would be in order. The bad feeling -
Is only part of the pain; however exemplary
The form has been drawn from suffering,
Is pain's benefic and malefic.
Scrutinize the scars, point by point,
They are yours, they are mine.

Concert: Leeds Town Hall

Light bleeds the windows white
Even the yellow electric pumps
Whiteness over a single bald pate,
Streaming white light everywhere
Which cannot break. April scattering
Pellicles of snow, inside, the piano
Shredding pellicles of sound. You ask
'Who iced the organ's white piping,
Fringed it with blue like a cake?'

Gilt for angels, black for orchestral shrouds;
Below the bright provincial brasses beam and gleam,
Whiteness, whiteness, everywhere the colour of sound
Mahler black, Wagner red gold and purple.
Green for Fauré but what's to match
Delius' rising and falling harmony?

You've got to get inside for that, inside
That single bald orchestral pate
Streaming white light breaking
Pellicles of sound into colour,
Shattering windows of coloured bubbles
Floating in white light – red primarily
Thumping blood, green for movement,
Gold, gold for harmony.

My Perfect Rose

At ten she came to me, three years ago,
There was 'something between us' even then;
Watching her write like Eliot every day,
Turn prose into haiku in ten minutes flat,
Write a poem in Greek three weeks from learning the alphabet;
Then translate it as 'Sun on a tomb, gold place, small sacred horse'.
I never got over having her in the room, though
Every day she was impossible in a new way,
Stamping her foot like a naughty Enid Blyton child,
Shouting "Poets don't do arithmetic!"
Or drawing caricatures of me in her book.

Then there were the 'moments of vision', her eyes
Dissolving the blank walls and made-up faces,
Genius painfully going through her paces,
The skull she drew, the withered chrysanthemum
And scarlet rose, 'Descensus averno', like Virgil,
I supposed.

Now three years later, in nylons and tight skirt,
She returns from grammar school to make a chaos of my room;
Plaiting a rose in her hair, I remember the words of her poem -
'For love is wrong/in word, in deed/But you will be mine'
And now her promise to come the last two days of term,
"But not tell them", the diamond bomb exploding
In her eyes, the key left 'Accidentally' on my desk
And the faint surprise.

The Vandal

Someone has been tearing up the autumn,
Its ripped leaves ripple across the road
Flip liked hinged cards in the moist grass.
The rain-varnished houses vanish in smoke,
Drift on the air like blown-out breath in gusts:
So we forget frog-ponds and nut-gatherers,
Remember instead that weather's for us
Who know too well its intentions, wind-keen,
Intense as the first frost hardening
Stubble grass to a tacky ice-blanket
Listen! In bed we hear the swollen trees totter,
Dropsical-limbed, murmuring outside the window
Like Catherine's insistent ghost-voice
"Let me in, let me in!"

Crosscurrents
(1970)

The Cardinal Looks Back

I was a good father to my people,
Their houses among the terraced hills
Adored God every day, grape-clusters on the vines
Made Christ's blood richer in the goblet
My father gave me: the chased silver had vines
Round the stem and Cellini made it,
'Let him take it to Rome', he had said,
'The Pope will adore it.' The backs of my people
Bent as I held it aloft with the Host,
The silver blazed in our eyes like the sun,
Their lips were cracked as they sipped
The delicate wine, the crook of my finger already
Held the ring of a Bishop but I would not go;
'When the harvest is over', I said, let me bless
The gathered grapes, I love to watch the purple juice
Flowing from under their feet and the feast after.
But my father called, I left my people
With a sot who embarrassed the Bishop.
I was not long in my see, two Popes died quickly
And my father's whispers never ceased, Rome called
And I was Cardinal at last. It is hot, fever-ridden,
No-one dare speak for the ears of spies;
I toss at night in my high room through my window
The villa'd hills, my private chapel has the goblet,
I hear my people starved in a famine,
Their harvest blighted for three years.

Together

for Brenda

Your blue dressing-gown
Lying on the chair back
Like a tired arm.

Waiting

I am waiting for the sky to flower
Like poems in a winter mind.

The Colossus

(*Goya, an old man in exile, looks at his self-portrait*)

A bull's neck, still much needed,
Deserving exile or the guillotine,
'Because you are an artist we forgave you',
Thus his royal highness gave thanks,
My fingers itching for brush and canvas,
Floury cheeks and rouge, legs a donkey would be ashamed of,
A wife who's been to bed with everything in Madrid.

First I was 'untalented', then 'mad and deaf'
Still I painted, my pain drew me on,
My kingdom had majas nude or veiled
Always with dark eyes like her
Whom I loved and they poisoned,
Duchess of Alba, dressed in silver grey,
A white pekinese at her feet with the world:
On the sand my name with hers
And 'always.'

Old men easily grow afraid;
Spain and her blood are distant.
Alba dead I paint my 'Milkmaid of Bordeaux'
In lingering silver-grey.

For the Day after Christmas

I let the darkness come, watch the room go
From shade of mid-afternoon to evening,
The polished surfaces reflecting darker and darker
Shadows, the fire bar glowing more redly bright.

I can no longer see the vapour of breath
On the air, I lean back from my open book
To let the pages gather what is left of the light.
The purple of the ink is royal and deep,
I let it trail across the page like an emperor's cloak.

Still and All

Creatures are still in the incandescence of being
Flames swathe but never burn stillness,
The moving hand makes in silence:
Brancusi's 'Sleeping Muse' most memorable
For the quality of repose, Chirico's
Sad stations breathe the life of absence.
Goya's Infant Don Manuel, 'Cinnabar against cool grey.'

Waking

Wires toss in the wind, shrubs flap
And the tap on windows wakes us
To March's mistral madness:
I see white crocuses amid the rain.

Letter I

Go seek Prince Charming in another place,
His is one face I shall not wear again
You would not have the stars for diadem.

Snow

There would be patterns in this
For some, its surface incredibly
Diamonded; feel it sliding underfoot
Moist like the slant vagina's tunnel.

Himself, When Young

Of all the odds and ends
Encountered on stations
With their stains and smells
Running in all directions,
What startled me into the past
Was the man with the waxed moustache.
It took me back ten years
To a room with a sepia portrait
On a wall posing a man
With waxed moustache, flower
Buttonhole and natty cane
Who sat beneath a portrait
Of himself, when young,
In a sunless room
Staring into the fire,
Under the glare
Of the oven's brass eye.

Vocation

I would with firm but delicate hand
Draw the snowscape, Japanese white,
Take from Hiroshige the grey birds
Held in a winter sky.

Making Love

Light on my lashes, light in your eyes,
Light from the watching stars:
Think of the dark, stretching to distances,
Touched by stardrift and the waiting moon.
Taste air in the morning
Warmed by the sun, finger
Dusk, pink and magenta, smell
Summer in buttercup yellow.

Mermaid hair falling like sunlight
    In a faun's afternoon,
Star-fall, sun-dark, moon-dust
    Of all my dreams.

Elegy

Bright sunlight makes me weep,
Sky so full of tears I draw to me,
Pavements, unloving, walk over me,
Fullness of a thousand faces.

The mornings are how days end,
He will wake me with love,
Faded, invading the peace,
I answer but inside the rash spreads.

Names, places is how they get me
Gathered in one tiny room they erupt,
Rain makes me laugh:
It hazes the day till I can stand
The way it looks at me.

Crosscurrents

After the first understanding
One begins again as a stranger,
Stranger than the glances of a stranger
Are the glances one gives the contours
Of the face of a friend: how you wonder
As she sleeps, face pale as death in sunlight,
Flickering with shadows as the train goes,
Where those lines came from you never
Noticed before, what horizons beyond you
Her eyes rest on, what unknown god
Her lips move in prayer to - and that flush
In the cheek - is it guilt or love or the neutral sun
Burns brightly where your lips once moved?

Behind it all the thoughts most of all amaze –
Beyond silver and asking they travel
In a land which wholly rejects you.
From the crack of an eyelid or between breaths
When the lungs half-hesitate the soul
Has slipped away and you may never follow.
Behind dark glasses the closed eyes
Complete the circuit, a look one did not know
For sure the direction of is certainly inward now,
Wayward too perhaps, though of that one can never be sure.
As she wakes with a question one discovers an answer
To one's own doubts too, but the doubts, once raised,
Are with us for ever, the answer was wholly uncertain.

The Lights of Leeds
(2001)

Uncle Bob

Shell-shocked from Korea
A grenade that left him
The platoon's only survivor,
Put him in Stanley Royd
For thirty years.

He tailored there
And out on weekend leaves
He made and mended
Everybody's clothes,
Crying copiously
While he sewed.

When they cleared out
The chronic cases
Uncle Bob came home,
Shopping for Edna,
Doing the garden;
When the lodger left
Without a word, the police
Searched his room,
The garden shed,
Even the chest freezer.

Oesophageal cancer
Is very final.
John, his son, waiting
To take the house,
Departed for a month's fishing
Until it was all over.
As a last rite
They put him in the LGI

But I spoke to the houseman privately,
Pulling together the bits of a life
Wholly given over to others,
Fallen comrades, Edna,
The grandchildren
His pension went on.
The houseman agreed to speak
To the surgeon privately.

He was on the table
For nine hours
With a fortnight
In intensive care -
It gave him two years more.

Edna went first and
At her funeral John,
In frustrated fury,
Hit him over the head
With an empty fish tank.

When secondaries started
I was not told
And in the hospice
He barely lasted
His first weekend.

A Meeting with the Princess

It seemed hardly the place for an encounter with royalty
Just a family get-together in a terrace house in Bradford
High tea with a few stuffy aunts I hadn't seen for years
Their husbands in tow like lost dogs sniffing round for food
But she came all the same, ushered in politely as a friend
Of a friend or somebody's cousin twice removed though
Everybody was a bit put out at first except me so I got
Sat down next to her and started to chat but people would
Keep chipping in, especially the young men, definitely upper-class
Gate-crashers who kept scowling at her and she kept snapping
Back at them and I said, "There seems to be a problem to do
With suppressed anger, I feel" and even my own son, somewhat
Unrelaxed but a genuine Old Etonian nonetheless, looked a bit
Embarrassed at the kerfuffle, but he kept standing by me wearing
His tails and perhaps it was this that finally sent the young
Men on their way and I managed to get her out for a breath
Of fresh air in the street and eventually we found our way to
Peel Park. Nobody seemed to notice who she was or perhaps they
Were too polite to say or they thought she was another Diana
Lookalike anyway we had some peace at last and forgetting
Protocol I put my arm round her and said, "You're just ordinary.
Like everyone, even the Emperor of China, that's the secret of life.
If there is one" and she started to cry softly and still nobody
Noticed and then the people and the park and even Bradford itself
Melted away in her tears.

Wyther Park School Leeds Five

I stood there in front of forty-five faces
The first day of term, not especially fancying
"Exercises in Mechanical Arithmetic" and so instead
I read a poem from Kirkup in Japan, about Nijinsky,
Hand-written on a fan of rice-paper.

Thirty years later, taking a Sri Lankan girl
In search of her first job around London schools,
A Head-of-English announced "You wouldn't get away
With that now!" as though I had committed
A crime-against-society.

I remember sending the boys out to change for P.T.
While the girls changed in front of me,
Was it some kind of incipient voyeurism?
And Sheila, my genius-child-poet, about whom
Redgrove said, "Of course you are in love!"
Or was it the poetry, some kind of anarchy,
"He's quite mad about it and teaches nothing else",
The barely literate student teacher said.

Wittgenstein alternated between junior school teaching
And philosophy
Leavis ranted but read poetry inspirationally;
Twenty years later a stranger on a bus tapped my shoulder,
"What you taught me at nine got me two O'Levels,
That was all I ever got."

The Innocent Eye

I struggled through streets of
Bricked-up, boarded-up houses,
Mostly burned-out, keeping
To the middle of the road,
Watching the abandoned gardens
With here and there a house
Still lived in, curtained
Against the daylight and distantly
I saw the iron railings of the school
I'd taught in thirty years before.
The same brick buildings, hop scotch
Squares and rounders posts
And the sign, 'Welcome to Wyther Park
Primary School,' the wooden prefabs
Where I taught poetry nine till four
Replaced by newer prefabs of I don't
Know what, hidden in trees with
Thirty years more growth, one playground
Grassed over, with benches and tables
Like a pub garden, yet there was the same
Innocence still, my inner sense declared.

I sat on a stone seat by the bridge
Over the canal, watching the pylons
Stretching away to Kirkstall Forge,
By the steps to the railway where
Once the station stood that took us
Every year to Flamborough Head.

Textures

The grain of the exposed boards
Speaks through the wall of the years
We are back in our cottage
On the wind-swathed hills
Watching late winter dawns
Gather like kindled flame.

We are back with those winter dusks, -
The hyaline air hung in darkness
And a vale of stars, waking in blankets
Laid on bare boards, making a fire
From our dreams.

We are walking through mist
On snow-skirled roads, taking turns
On a swing in a deserted park,
Hearing the rhythmic clank
Of dripping links.

Again I see your smile
I have missed the long years since
Touching your fingertips
Before our exhausted sleep.

Memento Mori

What brought me to that place
The day before the demolition crew?
Three hundred miles from home, in Leeds,
I went to view 'my old school,' long
Changed into a store for worn-out desks,
Demijohns of ink, stacks of registers
And rubbers, even the odd cane.

From a distance I saw at once a change,
Slipping roof slates, reeling gates,
Broken glass on window-sills
Doors ajar, a grey wet teddy-bear
Face down on the littered yard,
A shifty-eyed man carrying out
Bulging cardboard boxes: "You're
From the council, sir, I know, I
Meant no 'arm, just 'elpin things
Along, some bits for mi kids."

I shook my head and smiled,
"I came here once, long ago,
What's going on?" and he replied,
"It's coming down, to-morrer, you'd
Best look sharp and go round while
You can" and so I went inside, past
Cloakrooms of child-sized sinks, smashed
Dripping taps and numbered racks of pegs
In black and corridors where smells of creosote
Lingered and white wall tiles here and there
Still stuck with sugar-paper murals of
"The Coronation of our Queen" with
Crowns of gold milk-bottle tops and
Carriages like coal-carts and gummed-on
Grass gone sere for 'atmosphere' all
Interspersed with shaky copperplated
Plaques. 'The Mall' and 'St. James' Palace.'

The hall seemed tiny now, that once had
Loomed so large - shrunk to toy-size almost
The stage where a blackboard I leaned on
Broken castors, hundreds of hymn books,
Worn and torn and splashed with ink,
Spilling over empty milk-crates and
A canvas screen with the tonic sol-fa
Curling round the edges.

The classroom doors' brass knobs had
Verdigris and the cupboard where I gave
Jean Croall her first kiss was missing;
I wondered where they had gone,
My friends of all those years ago,
Colin Moorhouse with his horse-shoe tie-pin
Whose hoarse, whispered revelation,
"I saw Betty Hunt's tits" caught a
Sudden silence and the whole class rocked
And Old King Cole suddenly had to leave,
His spluttered laughter seeping
From the corridor and Betty shouted back,
"You lying bugger."

The day the king died Smigger
Came round every class, grave-faced,
"Boys and girls, I have bad news,
Our king has died" and every face
Was shocked and still and Vernon Long,
Who usually only belched, said loudly
In the hush, " 'E were a good 'un, 'im"
And no public utterance of grief
Has ever matched Vernon's, then or since,
For simple spontaneity or truth.
In the end there was nothing
I wanted as a memento,
The pictures sealed in my mind
Like the air in Tutankhamun's tomb
When grave-robbers rolled aside
The phalanxes of guardian gods
In stone the round cupola of
Ellerby Lane School crashed down.

Children's Games

Come Whitsuntide the tally-men grew fat:
The poorest kids turned out in new blue
Worsted suits and matching caps, socks in
Scarlet plaid and mirror-shiny shoes so
When that special Sunday came they never
Missed a door to knock and say,
"Something for mi Whitsies, Mister, please"
And mostly people gave a tanner or a
Three-penny bit and felt all good inside.

The Fowlers had six boys and Jim was once
My mate but I didn't like his manners much,
He'd gozzle on the wall and wee behind wagons.
When Julie saw his cock he laughed and winked,
"So what?" he said, aged ten, and hefted it,
"Where's yours?"

His father liked a drink and every night
His mam and him went off down Hunslet Road
And left their six the key and came back
Signing late. Their dad once went off on his
Own but never came back: his hidden ulcer
Haemorrhaged and he spewed back seven pints
Of Tetley's best, some blood and enough guts
To leave him dead.

Jim's sorrow came in waves, for days he'd sit
And say, "'E only went to a birthday party and
'Ad one single drink" and other times he'd sit
And stare in silence. He was always loyal and
Once when someone from away passed our street
End and called me for my grammar school cap
Jim turned and said, "I go there, too, want to
Make something of it?" the menace of his five
Brothers heavy in the air

The Council gave his mam a bigger house
Up in the Fewstons but they couldn't pay
The bigger rent or fares and came back quick
Enough to chump for Bonfire Night, trailing down
Knowsthorpe for broken branches, past the water
Works, where Kevin Keogh climbed the fence:
When the foreman saw his torn outsize overcoat
He slapped his head until it rang, "Keep out
You fucking Irish twat!" That was before I'd
Learned to answer back so when Ma Moorhouse
Clumped out in her calipers to tell us off
I asked, "By what law should we leave?"

And when she bellowed back, "Our Pete'll do you
When 'e's 'ome!" Jim, not to be outdone, laughed
And yelled, " 'E's eighteen stone and couldn't
Bash a bean, the gozzle-bag."

When Margaret Gardiner came I left Jim and
He went with the older lads while I sat on
Margaret's mam's wall and made up stories.
Marlene joined up when we played 'Doctors
And nurses' and I was always the doctor and
Margaret the nurse and Marlene the patient
But Margaret would never change with Marlene
Who egged us on but I hung back when Marlene
Went off with the older lads and Margaret
For Whitsies wore her new mauve blazer and
I loved her deep, violet eyes and her mam
Had such a knowing look all summer long.

The Gift

We were three weeks
Into term, Sheila,
When you came
Through the classroom door;
Forty-four children
Bent over books,
Copying Roethke's
'The Lost Son.'

You wrote your
First poem on the 'Moses'
Of Michelangelo.
Words cut like stone.
I taught you Greek
But your painting of
'The Essence of the Rose'
Was pure Platonic form.

You drew the masks
Of Comedy and Tragedy
In perfect harmony.
Having seen neither;
So Socrates was right.
Those who have the Spirit's gift
Will one day find the light.

My Father

I had a father once, the records say.
He has gone away down the long avenue
Of death, on the hand-held minor no mist
Of his breath, his firm signature no more.
No more holding down his hat in the wind,
Running to catch the last post, he has gone
Beyond the wind-shaped stones on the high wall.

His breath in that final coma came steady.
Stertorous, the oxygen mask, the catheter,
The telephone call summons and night train,
The taxi over the moors, the charge nurse
With little to say but kind words.

I had a father once, the records say,
Who carried me on the cross-bar of his bike
Down Knostrop: we saw the white bells
Of bindweed crawling with ants
Strangle the rusty railings.

My father, a quiet man, never knew what
To say, which is why he was taken
And I was not told and the records say
It was pneumonia that took him
And I was not told why the anti-biotics
Were not given.

Letter to Michael Horovitz

It is time after thirty years
We had our Poetry Renaissance
Rise, Children of Albion, rise!

It is time after nightmares of sleep
When we walked the streets of inner cities
Our poems among the burnt-out houses
And cars, whispering compassion
To the addicts shaking and the homeless
Waking and those who have come apart
In the nowhere of today
Begging in stations
Sleeping in boxes.

It is time to find
Our lost, those children
I taught three decades ago
To paint on ceilings
With sticks of incense
Rainbows of silence
For John Cage
To write on walls
In luminous paint
Pink haiku
For Allen Ginsberg.

It is time to awaken and emblazon the sky
With symphonies of sorrow,
To draft the articles of war.
Poets of the Underground
The doors have opened
The ghost of Walt Whitman
Grey-bearded, in lonely anguish
Walks with us.

The First Month of the Year

A page of the 'Kelmscott' Chaucer
Seen through our cottage window
When the Pennines were blind with snow
Flurrying round the stones.
The fire was low when I began to blow
That single flicker to a flame,
Was I too late, I wondered, the 'poet in name'
Whose mind runs endlessly
As fingers through an old man's hair?
(Either way I thought of you and your being there)

A portrait by Velasquez
Seen through the months of silence, vivid
As the door I painted scarlet for our love
When the wind joined us walking the moors;
The sculpture of Brancusi's Sleeping Muse
Seen against the sadness is more eloquent
Than the sun: there is something I would waken
Other than that ageless sleeper, if I dare,
(The way I dream of you and our being there)

Winterlight

Let us, this December night, leave the ring
Of heat, the lapping flames around the fire's heart,
Move with bodies tensed against the light
Towards the moon's pull and the cloud's hand.
Arms of angels hold us, lend our bodies
Height of stars and the planets' whirl,
Grant us sufficiency of light so we may enter
The twisting lanes to lost villages.

So we may stare in the mirror of silent pools
By long-deserted greens, deepen our sight
Of what lies beyond the things that seem
And make our vision clear as winterlight.

Leftovers

Empty chocolate boxes, a pillowcase with an orange at the bottom,
Nuts and tinsel with its idiosyncratic rustle and brilliant sheen
And the reflection in it of paper-chains hand-made and stuck with
Flour-paste stretching from the light-bowl to every corner
Of the room, Father Christmas himself was plastic
And his vast stomach painted red with a bulging sack
Behind his back and he was stuck in the middle
Of a very large cake. The icing was royal and you could see the
Whites of many eggs in the glister of its surface and on the
Upright piano the music of Jingle Bells lay open.

With aching hands I wrote thank you notes for socks
To sainted aunts and played on Nutwood Common
With Rupert until Tiger Lily's father, the Great Conjuror,
Waved his wand and brought me home to the last
Coal fire in Leeds, suddenly dying.
I got through a whole packet of sweet cigarettes with pink tips
Dipped in cochineal and a whole quarter of sherbet lemons
At a sitting and there was a full bottle of Portello to go at,
The colour of violet ink and tasting of night air and threepenny bits
Which lasted until the last gas-lamp in Leeds went out.

I had collected enough cardboard milk-tops to make a set of
Matchstick spinners and with my box of Rainbow Chalks
Drew circles on my top, red, white and Festival of Britain
Blue and made it spin all the way to the last bin-yard in Leeds
While they pulled it down.

I was a very small teddy-bear crouched on a huge and broken chair
Ready to be put out into the wide world and my mother was there
To see me off. The light in her eyes was out, there was no fire
In her heart and the binyard where I played was empty space.

Tranquillity Street
(2004)

Pulled from a Life Some Leaves

Pulled from a life some leaves in evergreen
Or dressed like fragrant crinoline draped
Over shadows by di Chirico, stolen
From a station where trains never run
And set up in a tableau in the parsonage at Haworth
The three sisters with Chekovian overtones
Stood round the table where their mirrored forms
Await the blast of the last judgement's call to make them
Take that final walk across the heather mantled moor.

Down vain corridors I searched for some leaf token
Of a life unlived, a faded mignonette or four leaved clover
Down a pathway closed forever by the twists of fate:
The shadows of you gone still took the night
And I was left alone to face the painful light.

Song for Mayday Morning

An alcoholic schizophrenic father
And an Irish immigrant mother who died when Brenda was fifteen
But still she managed to read Proust on her day off
As a library girl, turned down by David Jenkins,
'A rising star of the left' for a place at Leeds
To read theology started her as a protest poet
Sitting out on the English lawn, mistaken for a snow sculpture
In the depths of winter.

Her sit-in protest lasted seven months,
Eight hours a day, her libellous verse scorching
The academic groves of Leeds in sheets by the thousand,
She called the VC 'a mouse from the mountain';
Bishop of Durham to-be David Jenkins a wimp and worse
And all in colourful verse while 'Guntrip's Ghost'
Went to every VC in England in a single day.

When she sat on the English lawn Park Honan
Flew paper aeroplanes with messages down and
And when she was in Classics they took away her chair
So she sat on the floor reading Virgil and the Chairman of the
Department sent her an official Christmas card
'For six weeks on the university lawn, learning the
Hebrew alphabet'.

In Oxford Magdalen College school turned our son away
So she started again, in Magdalen Quad, sitting through Oxford's
Worst ever winter and finally they arrested her on the
Eve of the May Ball so she wrote 'Oxford from a Prison
Cell' her most famous poem and her protest letter went in
A single day to every MP and House of Lords Member.
It was remembered years after and when nobody nominated
Her for the Oxford Chair she took her own and sat there
In the cold for almost a year, well-wishers pinning messages
To the tree she sat under - "Tityre, tu patulae recubans
Sub tegmine fagi" and twelve hundred and forty dons had
"The Pain Clinic" in a single day and she was fourteen
Times in the national press, a column in "The Guardian"
And a whole page with a picture in the 'Times Higher' -
"A Well Versed Protester"

Ecoutez la voix du vent – listen to the wind's voice
As Milosz commands "All your griefs,
My sad ones, are in vain" but offering
In recompense soaring sonatas which remain unread
Untranslated, relegated to the reserve stock
Of the Institut Français, along with Fargue,
Jacob and Larbaud while all those Bloodaxe deadheads
Blossom and bloom round poetry's tomb
Where still there's room for Ursula's
Queen's Medal for Poetry, lacklustre poetaster.

To My Wife

1

You buy my freedom with your love.
With every book you catalogue or stamp
My imagination hacks a strand from the hawser
That for three years has held it
In the grubbing estuary of mud and time.

Your early waking with tired eyes
And late return at evening, all
Contribute to the store of images
I love you for: the irony being
Your job is worse than mine
Your talent more.

2

I do not understand myself, the time, or you.
I cannot comprehend our love, shot through
Like flying silk with flashes of gold light
And the tattered backcloth of suffering.
Each night I remember our meeting;
My hair 'like iron wire', the grey dust
In the air of my house, the exact place
On the carpet where I kissed you
And how we talked on and on,
Too much in love for love,
Until the night was gone.

3

We acted out our love
By nearly going mad,
Gave up the jobs we had
To take a cottage on the moors
At less than garage rent.
For food we learned to pledge our dreams
And found, too late, the world redeems
What it had lent.
By night the world unpicked
The dream we wove by day,
Each dawn we woke to find
The stitching come away.

4

Two creatures from a bestiary
Besieged our dream:
A neighbour's one-eyed cat
That prowled outside to bring
Its witch-like owner
With her tapping stick.
Was the Bach we played too loud for her deaf ears,
Or was it our love that howled her silence home?

5

We have re-built that house
With blood.
We have sculptured that dream
In stone.

Windsong

I drowse and dream in this sleeping house
Fynbos the cat purring by the curtain
Suriya the sun god sharing the garden
Where joss sticks burn and my nostrils quiver
At the echo of Japanese songs, long ago.
In the breaking day I kiss your lips
And taste the tongue of your waking shadow.

To the Memory of My Mother

This is one spring you will not see.
The fifty roses of your spray
Smelt soft across that February day
Where trees, heavy as only crematoria
Can bear, sloped down the fallen banks
To where we waited in the chapel, me
Clutching Father Kevin's hand, remembering
My given grace and faith renewed
In answer to my prayers, Brenda in tears,
And Joyce the sister of my years, Kim
And the others from the Home, where five
Long years you waited for this day,
Of all, the most important. Visits, letters,
Phone calls far too few, until we knew
When your last days began and for sixteen
Hours we sat, but still your will to live
Went on until our backs were turned
And then you, too, had gone.

The Play House

We had a new house
And split the decorating.
You took the piled rolls of paper,
While I stacked the cans of gloss,
One to each corner-white-what else?
And when we began our slow labour
We did not even sigh except in some relief
In being there at last.

There were no spaces for our children's visits
Nor for the children they would never bring.
All rooms sat square and small, but with
Every outside wall a window. There was light
Enough for a studio wherever you went,
And for the tiny hall you chose
A glazed blue bowl of your own making.
The house stood on a hill, just a little
Inaccessible but, in view of our age, others
Had to be near and there they were, paired like
Dominoes in black and white, or chequer board
Squares with a neat red pillar-box
Anchored on the corner.

All the day of the moving I longed to be alone
With you; for the men in their old-fashioned aprons
To finish and be off and make space for you to squat
And with your nimble fingers light the one real fire
We had been allowed, so I could sit in my winged
Windsor chair and decipher the text of the flames
And savour the smoke before the up-draft caught;
And for a few days there might seem little to say,
The clay wet in the bin, the canvases heaped in the studio,
And the faces in our children's photographs
Stranger than strangers.

The Philosophers

Lavender musk rose from the volume I was reading through,
The college crest impressed in gold, tooled gold lettering
On the spine. It was not mine but my son's,
Jammed in the corner of a cardboard box with dozens more;
Just one box of a score, stored in a heap across my ex-wife's floor,
Our son gone far, as far as Samarkand and Ind
To where his strange imaginings had led, to heat and dust, some lust
To know Bengali, to translate Tagore, or just, for all we know,
Stroll round those sordid alleys and bazaars and ask for toddy
If it's still the same and say it in a tongue they know.

The Classics books lay everywhere around the flat, so many
That my mind grew numb. Heavy, dusty dictionaries
Of Mandarin and Greek, crumbling Victorian commentaries
Where every *men* and *de* was weighed and weighed again,
And then, through a scholar's gloss on Aristotle,
That single sentence glowed, 'And thus we see nobility of soul
Comes only with the conquering of loss'; meaning shimmered in
That empty space where we believed there was no way
To resurrect two sons we'd watched grow up,
One lost to oriental heat and dust, the other to a fate of wards.
It seemed that rainy April Sunday in the musty book-lined rooms
Of Brenda's flat, mourning the death of Beethoven,
Her favourite cat, watching Mozart's ginger fur,
His plaintive tone of loss, whether some miscreant albatross
Was laid across our deck, or bound around the ship,
Or tangled about whatever destiny we moved towards
Across that frozen sea of dark extremity; fatigued as if our barque
Had hardly stirred for all those years of strife, for all the times
We'd set the compass right, sorted through those heaped up charts
And with fingers weary and bleary-eyed retraced our course.
The books, a thousand books that lined the walls:
Plato's chariot racing across the empty sky,
Sartre's waiters dancing like angels on the heads of pins,
And Wittgenstein, nodding in his smoke-filled Cambridge den,
Dreaming of a school room in the Austrian hills and walks

In mountain air, wondering why he wasn't there.
We wondered, too, at what, if anything we knew, trying to sift some
Single fact that might elicit hope from loss, enough to get us through
Another year with other griefs to come, we knew. Some, by a little,
Through God's grace or chance or simple will, we might delay.
More likely we would have no say. By words or actions
Who can stay the rolling balls across the table's baize,
The click of ball on ball, the line of bottles in the hall?

We heard the ticking of the Roman -figured clock
My mother made us take when all was lost,
Together until the last breath had flown
Into the blue empyrean with her soul.

Hughes' Voice in my Head

As soon as we crossed into Yorkshire
Hughes' voice assailed me, unmistakable
Gravel and honey, a raw celebration of rain
Like a tattered lacework window;
Black glisten on roof slates,
Tarmac turned to shining ice,
Blusters of naked wind whipping
The wavelets of shifting water
To imaginary floating islets
On the turbulent river

Glumly he asked, "Where are the mills?"
Knowing their goneness in his lonely heart.
"Where are the mines with their turning spokes,
Lurking slag heaps, bolts of coal split with
Shimmering fools' gold tumbling into waiting wagons?
Mostly what I came for was a last glimpse
Of the rock hanging over my cot, that towering
Sheerness fifty fathoms high screed with ferns
And failing tree roots, crumbling footholds
And dour smile. Monuments needs to be known
For what they are, not tourists slots or geological strata
But the dark mentor loosing wolf's bane
At my sleeping head."

When the coach lurches over the county boundary,
If not Hughes' voice then Heaney's or Hill's
Ringing like miners' boots flinging sparks
From the flagstones, piercing the lens of winter,
Jutting like tongues of crooked rock
Lapping a mossed slab, an altar outgrown,
Dumped when the trumpeting hosannas
Had finally riven the air of the valley.

And I, myself, what did I make of it?
The voices coming into my head
Welcoming kin, alive or dead, my eyes
Jerking to the roadside magpie,
Its white tail-bar doing a hop, skip and jump.

Leeds 1

1

O my beloved city,
How many times have I deserted you
For the sights and sounds of Babylon?
How often and from how far
Have I conjured your broad boulevards
O Quartier Latin, crowded street cafés
With white and scarlet awnings, gold
Adornings on stone cupolas, Byzantine domes
And plinths of equine statuary before
The Gare du Nord, grumbling fading
Faience of the Gare de l'Est?

Often, O how often, did I mingle with your crowds
Crossing the Pont Mirabeau in their Sunday best,
Regretting my lost loves, watching the barges
Snail along the Seine, hearing the bells
Of the Angelus dawn?

2

Exiled in the south and in a new century,
I recall leisurely Sundays on the Grande Jatte;
The children in sun hats knelt by their boats
Unfurling handkerchiefs for sails and for supreme farewells
(Shall I return? Steamer with your poised masts
Raising anchor for exotic climes?)

3

The bells of Sacré Coeur shake rickety tables
Where old men in blazers sport the Légion d'Honneur.
Priests in birettas sip Green Chartreuse over their
Breviaries while Wilde and Gide stroll round Père
Lachaise vying to outdo each other's tinted
Memories of soft-skinned Moroccan boys.

Weary of their weariness and of my own, and of
Rimbaud and Verlaine's battle of strophe and
Anti-strophe and rhetoric's demise, I take a
Lacquered tram to the Bois de Boulogne, hoping
To catch Mistinguette's last song.

To Brenda Williams on her Fiftieth Birthday

The years become you as Oxford becomes you,
As you became Oxford through the protest years;
From Magdalen's grey gargoyles to its bridge in May,
From the cement buttresses of Wellington Square
To Balliol, Balliol in the rain.

The years become you as the Abbey Road becomes you,
As you became that road through silent years,
From the famous crossing to the stunted bridge
Caparisoned with carnivals of children,
Cohorts of coloured clowns and Father Christmases.

The years become you as the Clothworkers' Hall in gold
Became you, and you became it through the protest years,
When the Brotherton's Portland stone, its white stone
Of innocence was snow in the School of English garden,
'A living sculpture', a *Grene Knicht* awaiting spring.

The years become you, Oxford, Leeds and London,
As you became them through the years of poems,
Through passing, silent crowds, through the cherry blossom
You sat under, plucked and ploughed, 'a dissenting voice',
And Balliol, Balliol in the rain.

Hymn 1

How I love the working-class girls of Leeds,
Their mile-wide smiles, eyes bright as beads,
Their young breasts bobbing as they run,
Hands quick as darting fish, lithe legs
Bare as they scramble over the Hollows
With brown-soled feet and dimpled bums
Half-covered with knickers, and short frocks
Full of flowers and their delicate ears,
Perfect teeth and flickering tongues, the
Fragile bones of their cheeks, the soft
Sweetness of their soprano voices dying
Away into the unforgotten magenta and
Yellow-ochre of innumerable twilights.

Lament

How I loathe this land of my exile,
Concrete upon concrete,
Steel upon steel,
Glass upon glass
In massed battalions
And no way back.
My mind moves to a far-off place
To a hill-top where the wind is my succour,
Its blow and howl and rage
Over the springing turf and heather
Calms as the song of a mother
And the last light's glimmer.

The Road to Haworth Moor

for Brenda Williams

1

The dawn cracked with ice, with fire grumbling in the grate,
With ire in the homes we had left, but still somehow
We made a nook in the crooked corner of Hall Ings,
A Wordsworthian dream with sheep nibbling by every crumbling
Dry-stone wall, smoke inching from the chimney pot beside the
Turning lane, the packhorse road with every stone intact that bound
The corner tight then up and off to Thurstonland, past the weathered
Walls of the abandoned quarry, beyond Ings Farm where Rover ran
His furious challenge to our call.

We had little, so little it might have been nothing at all
The few hundred books we'd brought and furniture bought
At auction in the town, left-overs knocked down to the few pounds
We had between us, dumped outside the red front door by the
Carrier's cart; stared at by neighbours constantly grimacing
Though the grimy nets of the weavers' cottage windows, baffled
As to who we were and how and why we'd come there.

I never gave it a thought (perhaps I should have) but with
The sense of 'poet' in my soul, a book to read and one
To write, night walks in the valley's hyaline air through
Brambled woods and on down tracks we trekked along
Until the sharp sneck of dawn drew us back to the
One-up one-down cottage on the lumbering hill.

Was it folly, chance or madness, another's or our own,
Drove us from Leeds, our native home, past shadows
Darker than death itself upon the bedroom wall
At Rawdon in the bungalow by the cross-roads where we met?
Three decades on and yet I cannot say for sure the destiny
That made us meet was dark or light, some sound or sight
'Beyond our mortal vision', some immaterial infinity,
A double helix on the heels of both that made my south
Your north and jerked the compass till we knew

Not day from night nor wrong from right.
Only a week ago you took me to the house you came from
Thirty years before. Together we stood as strangers in a room
Filled with plastic saccharine furniture, vinyl gloss, cabinets
Of china dogs and photographs of a departed wife and child.
All that remained of your family was a hidden coat of red paint
Beneath the kitchen windowsill and on a faded page the number for
Your long-gone neighbour, Lilly Clarke, ninety if she lives at all,
The memory of a lilac tree, the Anderson shelter
Hidden by the fence, and the incomer's invitation
To call again and then and then...

We were wrong from the beginning, you always said, wrong
To be together, wrong to go away or perhaps, as Hobsbaum said,
'It was the place's fault. If we'd made it to Haworth as we
Dreamed, standing on the moor top, the heather muffling your tears,
The wind sighing its threnody, crying its cradle-song, whispering
Promises of its care to come, its breath caressing the very stones
We sat on, lost beyond the ken of any guide, beyond the signatures
Of time and place, beyond, beyond...

2

There is no clock can measure what we both passed through,
The darker griefs that soon began to haunt your fragile sleep,
The echoes of nightmare flights through empty streets that soon
Began to creep behind the wainscot of those tiny rooms, the rat
That took them up and ran to hide and haunt us, encountered
At the cellar-head or heard beneath the boards. The sad rat-catcher's
Nod and shaking head, as if he knew more than the pair of us
What lay ahead. Like Charlotte's your hair lay in dark ringlets
On the pillow while I lay stunned and terrified and lost.
From then till now, two children grew, two fathers died;
One mad, one sad, but both alone. Together or apart our lives
Have changed beyond repair, the text altered and the cover bare
But still the same story more or less, echoing down
hospital corridors,
Left in faded waiting rooms and lost like our children,

Cyril Williams, gravedigger at Killingbeck, buried among
The graves his own hands dug, lay beside your mother,
'In death as in life together,' - what parody lies hidden
Beneath the marble chips of the unmarked grave?
Where is the cross of weathered wood and stapled names?
The thirty roses that you left had withered on the stem,
The weeds had spread and spread and you yourself
Were paler than the dead.

There may be little time or time enough for ills
We have to bear for others with our own. Madness
Seems our calling, yours and mine, speaking a tongue
Where words are symbols, signs and symptoms, pointers
To a buried past, clues to an untold murder.
Those nightmares came to haunt us and teach us and take us
To that room in Stainmore Place, your mother's ghost
At Banquo's feast, the guest that never could be laid to rest.

3

One stifling July day thirty years on we returned to Honley
Where the hamlet snagged on the hillside, fattened now and hollow
And grown grey with money and success: one cottage joined on
To the next, the common land fenced off, the nearby chapel
Turned to a desirable residence, the tombstones garden ornaments,
The heart of Hall Ings Mill crumpled under mechanical hammers
And reeled before our eyes, dust rising to powder the wings
Of passing butterflies. We watched the white-glazed inner walls
Sink in shame to shattered heaps of stone and shards of nothingness.

I never thought it would be the experience it was-
How could anything be more banal than a visit to Oakes?
Twenty two Georgian semis from the sixties, brass coach-lamps
By glass front doors, irreproachable gardens,
The estate lodge's great oak doors opening to vistas
Of street on street, the fields and cattle gone.
We peered through the polished windows at the hearth
We'd sat around, our hearts numb, but then
A quiet came we had not felt for years, a lens of silence

Enclosed us, a single leaf fell at my feet.

4

The rat we tried to frighten, trap or poison, saw us off instead;
It seemed as if it grew beneath our very skins and circled
With our blood and hammered at our heads and leered from specks
Of fluff beneath the bed. The wainscot was the worst, it seemed
No whitewashed wall was free from cavities that wound behind
And joined another maze of runs that opened to the boards of yet
Another floor, until the tiny house had grown to one great rat-run
Vaster than the universe, where that single rodent
Gnawed and slithered to unsettle finally our fragile peace.

I did not want to go. You did. I could not stay alone. It was
The whispers said and never ceased, 'the beginning of the end'.
Now, thirty odd years on, I do not know at all;
No certainty is certain, no narrative, however neat, is sure.
I know how listlessly we tried again in Leeds, a tiny flat
With the white telephone that never rang
Next to the Christian Science Church
My sad grandmother trekked to with her cancer-ridden spine.
It was doomed from the start. The previous tenants
Had ended in divorce. If the certain salesman and his gleaming
Bride had failed to make it, how could we?

Our moves from Huddersfield and back became more frantic and
Our peace more fragile. You always felt lonely in the countryside,
While in Leeds I longed for open vistas cloud-masses
Over the blue chain of hills, the silence of the lanes,
The sheep bells and the endless walks. Was I in flight?
You had to ask but then as now I had no answer;
But it's the way I was, hating the clutter of the city,
Man en masse. I thought I needed a mate for a Platonic cave,
A companion for the Martello tower in Dublin Bay,
Whatever it was I never wanted you to go but go you did to stay.
The one became the two again, you shed your ring,
We had our son to share.

I read instead of writing, psycho-analysis became a faith of sorts,
A pastime then a passion I kept on with even
When my muse returned demanding me in dreams.
Our children grew, then you wrote, too, by candle
In the dark or by the breath of the midnight sea on Brighton beach.
You made the rat return so I could face it, retracing childhood's
Nightmare footsteps while you recalled the terror of countless
Nights and days until I understood the meaning of our parted ways.

5

If only we could go back to the cottage on the hill at Honley
Where the road sweeps gently under the bridge
Where trains never ran our voices still echoing
Round the cavernous walls the smooth moss clings to
And we are beyond the reach of the driving rain.

There is always the odd cottage no one can be bothered with
Where the lorries roar but when you look behind a random stream
Gurgles by an overgrown track with a gully of pebbles
And overhanging rock, the door still hangs on that rusty latch;
Your thumb might still make it yield, not in the *sturm und drang*
Of adolescence but in the quieter intimacies of shared grief.

The hills have not moved nor the clouds altered the stance
Of their lazy azure nor has the watery Pennine sun
Gone in before the swallows gather.

Perhaps I have lost that *jouissance*-and who would not
Given the tornadoes, undivined and undeserved that
Seized our lives in their burning fury,
Leaving us awake in a world of dark horizons and troubled days,
Our memory a cave of broken shards.

One death came when a brother and a mother gathered
so that a father
Might die opportunely and without succour in a hill-top hospital,
Lonely as a scarecrow and inaccessible on the moorland midnight,
Beyond the reach of all but death standing at the bed-head.

Similarly, your own father blundering 'into the Selby Road,
High on morphine' could only end in the same way.

These griefs were only too normal, as was my mother's death.
You wrote with such sad eloquence as you shared my vigil:
Nothing could be added to your lines.

And of it all and of what cannot I speak?
The silence in Gethsemane
The breaking of bread
The communion when the wine I drank
Made your cradle Catholic soul
Fret at my insouciance.

6

Waking early I felt my sixty years
The winters of childhood slipping and sliding
In my tired imagination, the icicles on the kitchen window,
The ashes scattered over paths in patches of grey and black.

We have so much to comprehend, too much for any mortal,
The madness of youth, so fierce, so compulsive,
The cocktails of alcohol and drugs, the quarrels
                                        with knives and guns
Entered into as lightly as love was once with us.

Our generation awaits the taste of death
With none of the anticipated solace,
No children's children visiting in spite of the spare room
Stacked with toys, with shelves of dusty books,
Baum's 'Magical Land of Oz'
Its spine laid bare, Mombi the witch, Dorothy and Toto
Gathered forlornly round the saw-horse, the scarlet and crimson
Of their Edwardian rig slightly ridiculous, the Gothic typeface
Evoking sepia prints of my father at five in a pinafore or seven
In a sailor-suit feeding the Sunday birds, my grandmother
Framed in a trellis of *mignonette,* the aroma fragrant still,

The violet stock lingering and re-kindling our first garden
The autumn we moved in, the rampant blossoms eager in the soil
Of my father's first sowing.

For us there was no garden, the cottage at Hall Ings
Had only a paved yard, with tufts of grass and lichen
The whole country round an abundance of hedges and ditches
Where dog-roses blossomed, meadows of cow-parsley,
Stiles to field paths, the weathered sign 'To Thurstonland'
We followed with hand-in-hand innocence,
Returning at sunset, our hands full of violets.

The garden at Oakes stayed barren, the bare soil
Cumbered with builder's waste, resisting our listless endeavours.
The jobbing gardener stirred Paraquat,
Muttering under his breath as he sheltered in the garage
From the sudden rain. He left the seeding to another day,
Left it too late to sow, grumbled as he turfed it the day
After our move with Brenda alone, scrubbing the boards.
She saw him scowl as he punched the limp turf
With his calloused hands, demanding payment,
Angry at her innocence.

Brudenell Road had no garden to speak of,
A couple of feet at the front with a broken wall
And the back bare and hard from children's play,
The privet was matted with shards of glass,
Worn tennis balls and broken toys,
So tattered I cut it back to the wall, I sat on the top step and read,
Watching the children play in the sand I'd trundled in barrow loads
From the builder's yard, a make-do sandpit
Which drew the whole street, West Indian, English and Asian
Built temples together. Our sandaled bearded neighbour
Was the first to complain, his teacher wife beside him,
The next-door French widow supporting,
"So numerous the children, n'est ce pas?"
Meaning "Don't encourage the Pakis, there are too many already."
Like thunder the row erupted, a streetful of shouting,

My voice the loudest, the yesses had it,
The children remained, our last real garden.

7

In Memory of Emily Bronte

Besieged, beaten and bruised
I had proved my oracle lied
There was no peace in poetry and flight.
Yet as I sat and watched the night
Gather in the shallows of heather
I remembered the steep stone streets,
The ginnels of my childhood,
The walls of Roman York.

On this last June day, hidden by a haze of walls,
I found a cottage so overgrown I had to part a mass of green
To touch the door, the window-panes opaque with dirt,
Sills choked with books,
A rusted letter-box, cracked lintel, lichened roof-slates caving in,
A 'Sold' board hammered firmly into place.

There was no solace in the parsonage, no solace there at all,
The staff found it odd, my wanting to park my heavy bag and trudge
    from room to room. The couch Emily died on,
So shabby and so faded, Patrick's hat and sticks
Like stage props, Mrs. Gaskell's escritoire so thoroughly bourgeois,
    Charlotte's crinoline evoking 'Ooh' and 'Aah'.

I sat outside the tourist shop, watching the families pass,
Still reeling from the news of our son's loss,
His life-in-death and death-in-life.

The crowds gone, the shops closed
I browsed over rock and lichen,
O sleeper in the earth
Would that you might listen.

Would that you waken and tell me
Why young girls' beauty no longer moves me?
Their innocent glances as they leap-frog or hand-stand
With such *jouissance* takes hold of me no more.
I watched a troupe of Keighley girls
Pass through a turnstile on their way
To clubs in Leeds last night.

One wore a veil tacked round with sequins
Like scruples on the hem: there is no beauty like that girl's
Who's naked feet touched heaven in their swirls.

Note: I use the word 'scruples' in its old sense
i.e. a weight of 20 grains.

A Hope for Poetry: Remembering the Sixties

There was a hope for poetry in the sixties
And for education and society, teachers free
To do as they wanted: I could and did teach
Poetry and art all day and little else -
That was my way.

I threw rainbows against the classroom walls,
Gold and silver dragons in the corridors and
Halls; the children's eyes were full of stars;
I taught the alphabet in Greek and spoke of
Peace and war in Vietnam, of birth and sex and
Death and immortality - the essences of lyric poetry;
Richards and Ogden on 'The Meaning of Meaning',
Schopenhauer on sadness, Nietzsche and Lawrence on
Civilisation and Plato on the Theory of Forms;
I read aloud 'The Rainbow' and the children drew
The waterfall with Gudrun bathing, I showed
Them Gauguin and Fra Angelico in gold and a film
On painting from life, and the nude girls
Bothered no-one.

It was the Sixties -
Art was life and life was art and in the
Staff-room we talked of poetry and politics
And passionately I argued with John. a clinical
Psychologist, on Freud and Jung; Anne, at forty
One, wanted to be sterilised and amazingly asked
My advice but that was how it was then: Dianne
Went off to join weekly rep at Brighton, Dave
Clark had given up law to teach a 'D' stream in the
Inner city. I was more lucky and had the brightest
Children - Sheila Pritchard my genius child-poet with
Her roguish eye and high bright voice, drawing skulls
In Avernus and burning white chrysanthemums, teasing me
With her long legs and gold salmon-flecked eyes.

It was a surprise when I made it into Penguin Books;
Michael Horovitz busy then as now and madly idealistic
As me; getting ready for the Albert Hall jamboree,
The rainbow bomb of peace and poetry.

Bride of the Wind

for Brenda

Both had come with no gardener but the soul;
I had myself expressed them in weariness,
Like the last drop of milk from your tired breast.
The red rose was no rose for me.
My black rose shone in a silver dawn
In the throat of the wind.

On the tongue of the wind
I taste your spirit;
I will bear you on my toes
To the roof of the world.

February 1973

Note: This poem was inspired by Oskar Kokoshka's painting 'Bride of the Wind'

Requiescam

Let there be grass and trees to blow
And fold me in their shadow
Branches to shake and leaves
Turn brown, fall and lie fallow.
Let there be moorlands swept by wind
And raked by rain, purple splashes of heather
In autumn and sturdy boulders our forefathers
Carved their names on, emerald and slippery with moss
And pebble-strewn sheep-tracks crossing ditch and dyke
Where sudden rills of hill water strike free from
Hidden meanderings with the splash and rush
Of sudden laughter.

Let me lie with the sighing wind for choir,
Moss and lichen my only cover
When my earthly days are over.

A Memory at Sixty

They have vanished, the pop men with their varnished crates
Of Tizer and dandy, American ice-cream soda
And one percent shandy. The clunk of frothy quarts
Dumped on donkey-stoned doorsteps
Is heard no more, nor the neighs of restless mares
Between the shafts. The shining brass of harness
Hangs in bar-rooms or droops from imitation beams.

Gelded stallions no longer chomp and champ
In stalls beneath the slats of shadowed lofts with straw-bales
And hay-ricks as high as houses lazing in lantern light.
The ashes of the carts they pulled have smouldered into silence,
The clatter over cobbles of iron shoes and shouts of "Whoa, lass!"
Hushed in this last weariness.

To Brenda Williams ***Writing Against the Grain***

It was Karl Shapiro who wrote in his 'Defence of Ignorance'
How many poets go mad or seem to be so and the majority think
We should all be in jail or mental hospital and you
Have ended up in both places – fragile as bone china,
Your pale skin taut, your fingers clasped tight round a cup,
Sitting in a pool of midnight light, your cats stretched flat
On your desk top's scatter under the laughing eyes
Of Sexton and Lowell beneath Rollie McKenna's seamless shutter.

Other nights you hunch in your rocking chair, spilling rhythms
Silently as a bat weaves through midnight's jade waves
Your sibylline tongue tapping every twist or the syllable count
Deftly as Whistler mixed tints for Nocturnes' nuances or shade
Or Hokusai tipped every wave crest.

You pause when down the hall a cat snatches at a forbidden plant,
"Schubert, Schubert", you whisper urgently for it is night
And there are neighbours. The whistle of the forgotten kettle
Shrills: you turn down the gas and scurry back to your poem
As you would to a sick child
And ease the pain of disordered lines.
The face of your mother smiles like a Madonna bereft
And the faces of our children are always somewhere
As you focus your midnight eyes soft with tears.

You create to survive, a Balzac writing against the clock
A Baudelaire writing against the bailiff's knock
A Valéry in the throes of 'Narcisse Parle.'

When a far clock chimes you sigh and set aside the page:
There is no telephone to ring or call: I am distant and sick,
Frail as an old stick
Our spirits rise and fall like the barometer's needle
Jerk at a finger tapping on glass
Flashbacks or inspiration cry out at memory loss.
You peer through a magnifying glass at the typeface

Your knuckles white with pain as the sonnet starts to strain
Like a child coming to birth, the third you never bore.

All births, all babies, all poems are the same in coming
The spark of inspiration or spurt of semen,
The silent months of gestation, the waiting and worrying
Until the final agony of creation: for our first son's
Birth at Oakes we had only a drawer for a crib.
Memories blur: all I know is that it was night
And at home as you always insisted, against all advice
But mine. I remember feebly holding the mask in place
As the Indian woman doctor brutally stitched you
Without an anaesthetic and the silence like no other
When even the midwives had left: the child slept
And we crept round his make-shift cradle.

At Brudenell Road again it was night in the cold house
With bare walls and plug-in fires: Bob, the real father
Paced the front room, deep in symphonic thought:
Isaiah slept: I waited and watched - an undiagnosed breech
The doctor's last minute discovery - made us rush
And scatter to have you admitted.

I fell asleep in the silent house and woke to a chaos
Of blood and towels and discarded dressings
And a bemused five year old.
We brought you armsful of daffodils, Easter's remainders.
"Happy Easter, are you the father?" Staff beamed
As we sat by the bedside, Bob, myself and John MacKendrick,
Brecht and Rilke's best translator
Soon to die by his own hand.
Poetry is born in the breech position
Poems beget poems.

For James Simmons

Sitting in outpatients
With my own minor ills
Dawn's depression lifts
To the lilt of amitryptilene,
A double dose for a day's journey
To a distant ward.

The word was out that Simmons
Had died eighteen months after
An aneurism at sixty seven.

The meeting he proposed in his second letter
Could never happen: a few days later
A Christmas card in Gaelic - Nollaig Shona -
Then silence, an unbearable chasm
Of wondering if I'd inadvertently offended.

A year later a second card explained the silence:
I joined the queue of mourners:
It was August when I saw the Guardian obituary
Behind glass in the Poetry Library.

How astonishing the colour photo,
The mane of white hair,
The proud mien, the wry smile,
Perfect for a bust by Epstein
Or Gaudier Brjeska a century earlier.

I stood by the shelves
Leafing through your books
With their worn covers,
Remarking the paucity
Of recent borrowings
And the omissions
From the anthologies.
"I'm a bit out of fashion

But still bringing out books
Armitage didn't put me in at all
The egregious Silkin
Tried to get off with my wife -
May he rest in peace.

I can't remember what angered me
About Geoffrey Hill, quite funny
In a nervous, melancholic way,
A mask you wouldn't get behind.

Harrison and I were close for years
But it sort of faded when he wrote
He wanted to hear no more
Of my personal life.
I went to his reading in Galway
Where he walked in his cosy regalia
Crossed the length of the bar
To embrace me, manic about the necessity
Of doing big shows in the Balkans.
I taught him all he knows, says aging poet!
And he's forgotten the best bits,
He knows my work, how quickly
Vanity will undo a man.
Tom Blackburn was Gregory Fellow
In my day, a bit mad
But a good and kind poet."

I read your last book
The Company of Children,
You sent me to review -
Your best by so far
It seemed an angel
Had stolen your pen -
The solitary aging singer
Whispering his last song.

Incompatibilities
for Brenda Williams

La lune diminue; divin septembre.
Divine September the moon wanes.
Pierre Jean Jouve

Themes for poems and the detritus of dreams coalesce:
This is one September I shall not forget.
The school caretaker always had the boards re-blacked
And the floors waxed, but I never shone.
The stripes of the blazer
Were prison-grey. You could never see things that way:
Your home had broken windows to the street.
You had the mortification of lice in your hair
While I had the choice of Brylcreem or orange pomade.

Four children, an alcoholic father and
An Irish immigrant mother. Failure's metaphor.
I did not make it like Alan Bennett,
Who still sends funny postcards
About our Leeds childhood.
Of your's, you could never speak
And found my nostalgia
Wholly inappropriate.

Forgetting your glasses for the eleven plus,
No money for the uniform for the pass at thirteen.
It wasn't - as I imagined - shame that kept you from telling
But fear of the consequences for your mother
Had you sobbed the night's terrors
Of your father's drunken homecomings,
Your mother sat with the door open
In all weathers while you, the oldest,
Waited with her, perhaps
Something might have been done.

He never missed a day's work digging graves,
Boasting he could do a six-footer
Single-handed in two hours flat.
That hackneyed phrase
'He drank all his wages'
Doesn't convey his nightly rages
The flow of obscenities about menstruation
While the three younger ones were in bed
And you waited with your mother
To walk the streets of Seacroft.
"Your father murdered your mother"
As Auntie Margaret said,
Should a witness
Need indicting.

Your mother's growing cancer went diagnosed,
But unremarked until the final days
She was too busy auxiliary nursing
Or working in the Lakeside Café.
It was her wages that put bread and jam
And baked beans into your stomachs.

Her final hospitalisation
Was the arena for your father's last rage
Her fare interfering with the night's drinking;

He fought in the Burma Campaign but won no medals.
Some kind of psychiatric discharge- 'paranoia'
Lurked in his papers. The madness went undiagnosed
Until his sixtieth birthday. You never let me meet him
Even after our divorce.
In the end you took me on a visit with the children.
A neat flat with photographs of grandchildren,
Stacks of wood for the stove, washing hung precisely
In the kitchen, a Sunday suit in the wardrobe.
An unwrinkling of smiles, the hard handshake
Of work-roughened hands.

One night he smashed up the tidy flat.
The TV screen was powder
The clock ticked on the neat lawn
'Murder in Seacroft Hospital'
Emblazoned on the kitchen wall.

I went with you and your sister in her car to Roundhay Wing.
She had to leave for work or sleep
You had to back to meet the children from school.
For Ward 42 it wasn't an especially difficult admission.
My first lesson: I shut one set of fire-doors while the charge nurse
Bolted the other but after five minutes his revolt
Was over and he signed the paper.

The nurse on nights had a sociology degree
And an interest in borderline schizophrenia.
After lightsout we chatted about Kohut and Kernberg
And Melanie Klein. Your father was occasionally truculent,
Barricading himself in on one home leave.
Nothing out of the way for a case of that kind.
The old ladies on the estate sighed, single men were very scarce.
Always a gentleman, tipping his cap to the ladies.
There seems to be objections in the family to poetry
Or at least to the kind that actually speaks
And fails to lie down quietly on command.
Yours seems to have set mine alight-
I must get something right.

To Daisy Abey

In sleep I dream the gratitude I know I cannot say
Now you are in a latitude where palm trees hold the sway
There are always things between us that keep getting in the way
And stop me from expressing the things I mean to say
In a night of wind and weathers love will not go away.

A Fine Madness

Any poets about or bored muses fancying a day out?
Rainy, windy, cold Leeds City Station
Half-way through its slow chaotic transformation
Contractors' morning break, overalls, hard hats and harness
Flood McDonalds where I sip my tea and try to translate Valéry.

London has everything except my bardic inspiration
I've only to step off the coach in Leeds and it whistles
Its bravuras down every wind, rattles the cobbles in Kirkgate Market
Hovers in the drunken brogue of a Dubliner in the chippie
As we share our love of Joyce the Aire becomes the Liffey.

All my three muses have abandoned me. Daisy in Asia,
Brenda protesting outside the Royal Free,
Barbara seeing clients at the C.A.B.
Past Saltaire's Mill, the world's eighth wonder,
The new electric train whisperglides on wet rails
Past Shipley's fairy glen and other tourist trails
Past Kirkstall's abandoned abbey and redundant forge
To Grandma Wild's in Keighley where I sit and gorge.

I've travelled on the Haworth bus so often
The driver chats as if I were a local
But when the rainbow's lightning flash
Illumines all the valleys there's a hush
And every pensioner's rheumy eye is rooted
On the gleaming horizon as its mooted
The Bronte's spirits make the thunder crack
Three cloaked figures converging round the Oakworth track.

Haworth in a storm is a storm indeed
The lashing and the crashing makes the gravestones bleed
The mashing and the bashing makes the light recede
And on the moor top I lose my way and find it
Half a dozen times slipping in the mud and heather
Heather than can stand the thrust of any weather.

Just as suddenly as it had come the storm abated
Extremes demand those verbs so antiquated
Archaic and abhorred and second-rated
Yet still they stand like moorland rocks in mist
And wait as I do till the storm has passed
Buy postcards at the parsonage museum shop
Sit half an hour in the tea room drying off
And pen a word or two to my three muses
Who after all presented their excuses
But nonetheless the three all have their uses.

Memories of the Fifties

Eggshell and Wedgwood Blue were just two
Of the range on the colour cards Dulux
Tailored to our taste in the fifties,
Brentford nylons, Formica table tops and
Fablon shelf-covering in original oak or
Spruce under neon tubes and Dayglo shades.

Wartime brown and green went out, along with
The Yorkist Range, the wire-mesh food safe
In the cellar, the scrubbed board bath lid
And marbled glass bowl over the light bulb
With its hidden hoard of dead flies and
Rusting three-tier chain.
We moved to the new estate, Airey semis
With their pebble-dash prefabricated slats,
Built-in kitchen units and made-to-measure gardens.
Every Saturday I went back to the streets,
Dinner at Auntie Nellie's, Yorkies, mash and gravy,
Then the matinee at the Princess with Margaret,
The queen of my ten-year old heart.

Everybody was on the move, half the neighbours
To the new estates or death, newcomers with
Rough tongues from over the bridge slum clearance.
A drive-in Readymix cement works bruised the Hollows,
Ellerby Lane School closed, St. Hilda's bulldozed.
The trams stopped for good after the Coronation Special
In purple and gold toured the city's tracks and
The red-white and blue on the cake at the street party
Crumbled to dust and the river-bank rats fed on it
Like Miss Haversham's wedding feast all over again.

The cobbled hill past the Mansions led nowhere,
The buses ran empty, then the route closed.
I returned again and again in friends' cars,
Now alone, on foot, again and again.

Resurrection

I thought of my 'faculty of poetry'
As of the eye
The bream or white-bait showed
In its hysterical dance of death
When the receding tide
Left it asleep
In a shallow pool on the shore.

Why did I fail to take it?
Was I strangely compassionate
Or merely afraid to touch
The jerking spasm of flesh
With the still eye?

Or was it I on the shore
In the shallow pool, left by the tide,
Engaged in that mystic dance of death,
Twenty years before?

The Prism

Through the windows the sun's light
Turns to amber, the moon's to jade;
All night long I lie awake, wondering
How much your stunned heart can take.
That moment's 'sudden interminable splendour',
Our love kept up through the years of stress,
Strange dark-haired creature, the light over the water
Burns and beckons through our emptiness.

You

Remember, you loved me, when we were young, one day

The words of the song in Tauber's mellifluous tenor
Haunt my nights and days, make me tremble when I hear
Your voice on the phone, sadden me when
I can't make into your smile
The pucker of your lips, the gleam in your eye.

The day we met is with me still, you asked directions
And on the way we chatted. You told me how you'd left
Lancashire for Leeds, went to the same TC as me, even liked poetry
Both were looking for an 'interesting evening class'
Instead we found each other.
You took me back for tea to the flat in Headingley
You shared with two other girls. The class in Moortown
Was a disaster. Walking home in the rain I put my arm
Around you and you did not resist, we shared your umbrella
Then we kissed.

I liked the taste of your lips, the tingle of your fingertips,
Your mild perfume. When a sudden gust blew your umbrella
Inside out we sheltered underneath a cobbled arch,
A rainy arch, a rainbow arch.

"I'm sorry", you said about nothing in particular, perhaps the class
Gone wrong, the weather, I'll never know but there were
Tears in your eyes but perhaps it was just the rain.
We kissed again and I felt your soft breasts
And smelt the hair on your neck and I was lost to you
And you to me perhaps, I'll never know.

We went to plays, I read my poems aloud in quiet places,
I met your mother and you met mine.
We quarrelled over stupid things.
When my best friend seduced you I blamed him and envied him
And tried to console you when you cried a whole day through.
The next weekend I had the flu and insisted you
Came to look after me in my newly-rented bungalow.
Out of the blue I said, "What you did for him
You can do for me". It was not the way
Our first and only love-making should have been,
You guilty and regretful, me resentful and not tender.
When I woke I saw you in the half-light naked, curled and innocent
I truly loved you if I'd proposed you might have agreed,
I'll never know.
A month later you were pregnant and I was not the father.
I wanted to help you with the baby, wanted you to stay with me
So I could look after you and be there for the birth but your mind
Was set elsewhere and I was too immature to understand or care.

When I saw you again you had Sarah and I had Brenda,
My wife-to-be; three decades of nightmare ahead
With neither of our 'adult children' quite right,
Both drink to excess and have been on wards.
Nor has your life been a total success, full-time teaching
Till you retired then Victim Support: where's that sharp mind,
That laughter and that passion?

And what have I to show?
A few pamphlets, a small 'Selected', a single good review.
Sat in South Kensington on the way to the *Institut* I wrote this,
Too frightened even to phone you.

Summer Fever

The unsettled trees seem to share
My tensions of body and mind:
Unable to move before the shell of the wind,
Yielding as much as their nature allows,
They will break if pushed too far,
Splinter to show the white flesh of their wood
And sweet transparencies of sap.
If I am pushed too far I will show
The world our wounds, our nine months' child
In his robe of flesh and my wife's tired eyes;
We cannot sleep, alone or together, in case we conceive
Another like this, tearing us from the shell of our senses,
Bending our minds from their roots with his
Eighteen hour shifts of need.

For nine months we have worked through days
And nights; in the nine before his coming
When once you fell I felt his body scramble
In terror round the waters of your womb;
Only the placental coil stopping the leak
From life of his precious blood.

My Only Valentine

Your voice on the telephone
Hushes the storm in my heart
Lightning strikes twice
In the same place.

I cannot picture your face
No photograph, no keepsake,
No letters scented with your smile,
No ring or marriage bed.

Your kisses were the best
I ever had, my first,
My only valentine.

Directions/Misdirections

I sit inside the train of tears
The station mellow in shade
Unoriginal phrases air-brush the canvas.

Puzzling minds I wonder
If all are like my own,
Closed to stillness.

From girders hang the acrobats of gone
Pearl grey of Whistlers. We sat on
A train like this once, you and I,
Face to face but travelling
In opposite directions-
Or was it you alone I watched depart,
Stood on the platform edge, anxious and alert?

Letters to Friends

I
Brenda Williams

Leeds voices soothe the turbulence
'Ey' 'sithee' and 'love', lastingly lilt
From cradle to grave, from backstreet
On the social, our son, beat his way
To Eton, Balliol, to Calcatta's Shantiniketan
And all the way back to a locked ward.

While I in the meantime fondly fiddled
With rhyme and unreason, publishing pamphlets
And Leeds Poetry Weekly while under the bane
Of his tragic illness, poet and mother,
You were driven from pillar to post
By the taunting yobbery of society
And the crass insensitivity of wild therapy
To the smoking dark of despair,
Locked in your flat in the Abbey Road
With seven cats and poetry.
O stop and strop your bladed darkness

On the rock of ages while plangent tollings
Mock your cradled rockings, knock by knock.

2

Daisy Abey

Daisy, dearest of all, safest
And kindest, watcher and warner
Of chaotic corners looming
Round poetry's boomerang bends
I owe you most a letter
While you are here beside me
Patient as a miller waiting on wind
To drive the great sails
Through summer.

When the muse takes over
I am snatched from order and duty
Blowing routine into a riot of going
And coming, blind, backwards, tip
Over arse, sea waves crashing in suburbia,
Saturnalia in Sutton, headlines of mad poet
Striding naked over moors, roaring
"I am here I am waiting".

3

Jeremy Reed

Niagaras of letters on pink sheets
In sheaths of silver envelopes
Mutually exchanged. I open your missives
Like undressing a girl in my teens
Undoing the flap like a recalcitrant
Bra strap, the letters stiff as nipples
While I stroke the creviced folds
Of amber and mauve and lick
As I stick stamps like the clitoris
Of a reluctant virgin, urgent for
Defloration and the pulse of orgasm.

from The Nostalgia Bus
(2007)

November Fog

Seeing its grey pall fall over the roofs of Beeston
I remembered how in my childhood it would fall off the river,
A ball of freezing air to make a magic world where the glow
Of flickering gas lamps brought the echo of Hansom cabs
And chorus girls in silhouette with men in opera hats
While from the ruins of bombed-out Hunslet over the bridge
Of sighs rose from the silver air the thunder of a pianola's
'Come into the Garden, Maud', shuffling lamp-lighters with
Their fire-tipped poles, footfalls of factory girls
Rushing to turn up the gas when the knocker-up clashed
His ten-foot stick on their clammy windows, his hoarse cry
'Get thee up!' muffled by the shrouded bin-yards where
We tigged and played 'catch n' kiss',

Kirkgate Market Cafe

You can find anything here if you ask or look around
From liverwurst sausage to a 'Cambridge School' anthology;
The market holds me in thrall as James Kirkup before me,
Wreathe makers still, laughing Floras and unsure boys
Hosing down buckets of weeping carnations.

On a wall plaque the names of the city fathers
Brass rubbed to an illegible scrawled immortality
'Joe's Cafe Closed' blocks the steps up to the balcony
'Thank You Teacher' cards this week's speciality.
I'm glad to be alive, glad to be me, free of fame,
Free to sit and write pleasing no-one but myself
I wonder where they are, the friends of my childhood
The blurred grainy snapshots focus and fade:
I watch the shadows gather and lengthen, shade by shade.

The Storm

It was exciting, the storm,
I knew nothing but the sky's own demeanour,
A sudden shaking in the clouds
And a ripple of rain
While slates tacked house to house;
Awash with gold light the clouds
Lacquered the land mass.
A loose wind was banging the houses,
The slates of chapels were restless,

The pain and the sorrow,
Terror of darkness,
Lonelier moments:
The wind, the Pennines,
The distance.

Dies Irae

Summoning the ghosts of the dead
I do not dream of Caesar
But of you Uncle Arthur
In your greasy overalls,
Home from Hudswell Clarks
In Hunslet, copper-smith
Who helped to build
Tank engines for Ceylon,
Double-headers for the Veldt.

From fourteen to fifty-four
You never had a day off sick,
Your trips to Blackpool
Every Banky week were always
Blessed with non-stop sun
And Bamforths' postcards
Showed you shared the beach
With half of Leeds.

One day you came home early,
Sat fidgeting before the fire,
Smoking one Capstan Full Strength
After another; Auntie Nellie
Was working at the Maypole
So you told me, at twelve,
Your troubles, "They just went
Bust once gaffer died, his lad
Just couldn't thoil it, so we got
Our cards and that was that".

For months he moped, they told him
Copper-smiths were no more use,
"It's plastics now" and he was
Far too old to learn another trade
And then the Maypole folded too
When supermarkets came and Nellie
Stayed with you at home until
She dropped behind the door
And no-one knew for hours.
The hospital they took her to
Had wooden prefab wards; I visited
One Sunday afternoon, she held on
To my hands and kept on crying,
"Barry, tell your dad he's educated,
He'll know how to get me out".

She cried until she died
And Uncle Arthur lasted
Two years more; they knocked
The houses down and so he moved
But never bothered to unpack,
Dying in hospital during
A routine check.

The Vigil

I am always in attendance at the state
Lying-in hospital, at night in a side-ward
With a girl barely sixteen. Unmarried,
Ignorant, terrified in first labour,
She twists her hands together,
Watching the sweeping hands of the clock,
My own hand on her brow stroking
The dark curlicues of hair, damp with fear.

She has thrown aside the sheets to touch
The life beating within, outside is the nub
Of flesh, bare where they shaved her,
Dark with the brown line of birth.

Hesitantly she touches her breast, already swollen,
The bruised star of a rose areola: the head
Of her child, the miracle's shadow shows,
Soon I am washing him, bathing the tears from her face.
In exultation she touches his face, no longer a girl.

Fairy Tales of Leeds

1

Ben's cycle shop at Crossgreen had the odd few Christmas toys,
A clockwork Triang train in a grand cardboard box, on the cover
A boy in a red pullover glowing over 'The Coronation Scot'
Full-steaming ahead through glens and loch-laden mountain
Scenes and a sign 'To Edinburgh Fifty Miles'.
Waking, a few weeks later, to find the box bulging my Christmas
Pillowcase, I wound the green engine incessantly and put it
On the track but it always came off at the first bend.
I coupled up the chocolate-coloured carriages, sending it
Across the carpet till it hit the fender, crashing over
With its wheels spinning in the air, going nowhere.

2

In Mr Murray's papershop were boxes of string on shelves,
Penny ice lollies you sucked until the colour went, leaving
You with ice castles on sticks. Every week I bought two
Threepenny Sexton Blake mysteries, sixty-four action packed
Pages, full of rascally Lascars and pig-tailed Chinese devils.
There were twopenny packets of stamps for my Royal Mail Album,
Stately portraits of Sun Yat Sen, Gold Coast clippers, salt
Gatherers on a palm-fringed shore - 'Turks and Caicos Islands'.

3

Len the cobbler kept tacks beneath his tongue, a trick
He was taught at Cobblers' College; he said he could spit
Them straight into the leather but only without an audience
Whose eyes stopped the magic from working.

4

Up Easy Road was Rocket's Greengrocers - Stanley Rocket
Had a green van he took me and Colin in, delivering.
In Kirkgate Market Car Park the attendant shouted,
"On your way, sky-rocket, you're too mean to pay!"
Stanley laughed and parked anyway but he told us
To hush when we drove to the house of a Big Doctor
At the Infirmary. A snooty housekeeper took the box
Of fruit and veg in, sniffing all the way to the
Tradesmens' entrance.

Back at the shop on brass rails were clumps of bananas,
Tins of under-the-counter Grade 'A' salmon and their
Aunt Mary had her chiropodist's surgery over the shop;
When I got a verucca at the baths she scraped it away
Week after week till it bled into nothing.

5

Up Easy Road was the Maypole with its tiled tapestry of
Village Green, flower-decked maypole and dancing children
Like little Shirley Temples with bows in their hair and
Bows tied to their shepherds' crooks. There were biscuits
In boxes with glass tops and Mrs Hyde, the manageress,
Used to give me custard creams to persuade my mother
To be a Registered Customer but she wouldn't move from
Boring Rockets with their cheap bruised fruit.

6

When her mam called Margaret in 'To run an errand'
It was only me she took with her over the suspension
Bridge down Hunslet to the corner shop 'For a packet of
Dr. White's', Margaret whispered in my ear, touching the
Lobe with her tongue and her eyes shone.

The Break

Writing again after twenty-five years' silence
I found respect for my mentors less, almost gone:
Aiken, Roethke, Lowell seemed paler, thinner,
I'd see flaws where before I worshipped. Something
Had moved in my perspective and could not go back,
Experience had shifted things round - the razor of
Early morning mist, half-light, wakens the mystic
In me, place becomes memory.
Just being and moving
Make poems and sometimes dreaming; at six I sat
Before the fire, my toes teasing the rug, loading
A silver pencil with absorbed delight,
Reading 'The Coral Island'.

At nine, the class huddled over desks,
I ran to post my teacher's letter,
The city distant and deserted,
Aware of myself as the wind
Reaching to touch a blade of grass, my cheek.

Between home and school lay the Hollows,
A mile of wasteland where streets
Once stood - filled-in cellars,
Broken doorsteps
Under a tide of weeds.
The abandoned wharf ran by the riverside,
Warehouses empty for decades:
We stared into the warm darkness,
Bursting sacks of lime,
Nettle-beds, the road closed.

Lochia

1

Voyaging under the cool arc of midnight
On a ship that was a star
Or clinging to a broken spare
Where the jewelled archipelago sings:
Little peewit, little peewit, what's your name?
Little master, little master, Red Legs.

I am Louis Wain, madman and artist,
Famed painter of cats.

I am Pere Tanguy, my cellar full of Cezannes,
Sitting for Vincent.
I am myself, praising Whitman,
In forma pauperis.

2

Finch, finch, sing your green song
Out of the sky-roads
Your bright cousins come,
Snow, lazuli or painted
Buntings with plumes of flame.

3

Theseus took a thread
While I had none:
I spun a rope of crystal
And threw it at the sun.

Avenue des Hirondelles
To the walled garden
Where I could not go.

4

Butcher bird, butcher bird
Dive on the mocking bird
Fasten her wings
On the nails of a tree.
Gorge on the delicate
Meat of her mockery
Gouge out her eyes
So she cannot see.

My son's coloured ball
Is patterned with Saturn's
Nine moons: through the haze
Of a June day a golden
Oriole nests in an ebony tree.
When our son sleeps
My mind is rinsed
In the canals of Mars
Scarlet, orange and paradise tanagers
With plumes of stars.

Sounds at Night

In the successive layers of ether
Lie scattered the sounds of centuries,
From prehistory the trumpeting of mammoth,
The grunt of ur-man, the rending
Of ice from ice as glaciation
Came and went.

Like searching the sand on every shore
For one unique specimen of shell
You would look for history's zeniths,
Socrates conquering his stutter
Against the roar of the ocean,
Cleansing res publica
With the salt
Of his sea-wit.
Wisdom began with the oceans -
The roar and surge in the surf
Chorused Troy's doom,
Bore Ulysses landward
To Penelope and his Ithacan home,
Bears me through the space

To the stars, across the stained
Aeons of history
To the cries
Of the dying.

By the side of the few great
And the still more infrequent good
Lie the tears of millions,
Beside Cleopatra's last words to Antony
Stands the enormous agony of myriads.
I read of a foundling hospital
Half a century ago where no infant
Survived its first year, though
Given every care
But had to stare at a bare
Ceiling every moment of every day
And wore a hollow in his mattress
With lying still his first half year.

I stare through space and hear
Their cries alone at night
Untended, unheard, for evermore.

Mother Earth

Grains in the black earth grow
Fed by the sweet waters of other Earth
Greening the land.

I am at home, here, with the dawn
Or at dusk, but alone, always alone,
Longing for love.

In the night I am bent
Over the bed of a sick child
Or dying woman, hearing always
The beat of Mother Earth's heart,
The slow pulse of birth
With its not-to-be denied rhythm
Of emergence, like the first nova
Of a new constellation, altering
The maps of the stars.

I am at war, with the defeated
Army always, at a base hospital,
Watching the slow procession of stretcher-borne
Dead and dying, the cheap black uniforms
With crossed swords crying for a cease of blood,
Mounting through rungs of fever
To the footrest of the stars.

The Sense of Being

There is much of the woman in me, too,
Bearing poems
Pressing down
Till they
Come
Like a child slipping from the womb
Oiled with placental blood
Crying before he came.

It is the eternal in childhood
I miss most: my son's delicate features,
His smile.
In his fragile penis
His own death
His own son's seed.

But his laughter
Death cannot stifle,
Rhythmic like birth
Moment by moment
Appearing and disappearing
Creating, bearing down,
Crowning.

The Black Swan

Jet-feathered, expressionless,
Downward moving, I watched
A black swan glide
Through the streaming air
Of my mind: dead, but for
The almost imperceptible vibration
Of wings, with others before and after,
Limitless procession of black swans
On an invisible belt, stirring
The surrounding currents
Like the trembling air
Around a fire.

The mind has limitless fathoms,
Beyond lives easily gained and lost
And what they contain, there are
Mirrors of white light shimmering,
Love stretching beyond
The uttermost reach of the stars.

Such love and such lovers are gathered
Under the soft, protective feathers
Of the gleaming black swan
Gliding downwards through my mind.

Bound in a Cart

'And like a doleful tragedy
They bound him in a cart'
– 'Sir John Barleycorn'

Trussed, nowhere trusted,
You go forth in springtime:
Grief, mist, leaves splayed in the wind.

The children like to be alive, so far,
One at fifteen is elf-like still,
Already with her fill of pain.
I see through the thin dress
Her pale white body, the limbs
Lithe in love.
Most here are doomed,
The girls will be factory hacks, broken,
Hard-faced. A few boys have spirit,
The bosses will break it or tame it.
The school is a lewd
Mass of rules, the children a chaos.

Spain Redivivus

Reading Octavio Paz
I remember you, old Holmes,
My first and only
Teacher of Spanish,
Your arm trembling
From shell-shock,
Painful limp,
Grey hair shaken across
A furrowed brow
As you uttered "Atelante"
And at nine we poured
Into your room, walled
With posters of bulls
At bay, caped matadors
And picadors, sunny seville.
Your rages were famous
But I never believed them,
An old stager, never
Missing your cue,
Striding the classroom boards,
Your eyes heavenwards, your
Good arm raised in wrath
Never descending, your curious
Passion for Spain.

Beneath your shouting
And your show
I sensed some absolute.
You had not fought Franco
Or been six years in Africa
To ape your enemies.
Your desert paintings
Were legendary: years later
Another told me how once
You brought them out
At a leavers' party,
Hushing the room
With their eerie stillness
Of the desert midnight.

Uncollected

December

for Daisy

For you words aren't enough
For me they too numerous to read
In ten lifetimes. Though at sixty-eight
Late as it is I try, I try.

The whiteroaded silence beyond the windows
Of the Londonward leap of the train
Stirs memories of nineteen forty six
When drifts stood higher than your head
And made us dream eternities of snow,
Of Scott's Antarctica, of the glow
Of coals in my mother's black-leaded grate,
Platoons of pow's hefting shovels
To clear the snow-skirted roads.

An ivory tower, my childhood, no beatings,
No neglect, Meccano and Biggles, Marks and Spencer's
Angel cake, Boots book department in its Briggate basement,
Keats mock-Morocco bound, titled in silver,
My first kiss from Margaret forever
Lost in Seacroft.

My audience is entirely Stateside webs
Whisking my oeuvre *tout court* to a Latina
Who chose *This December Night* to light
In an Hispanic turn, Neruda's tongue,
O how I envy, how I envy him
Rosa del pubis, only he could grasp
The essence of the second sex.

The prison hall of secondary school, all boys
With Bennett about to go to Oxford
And become a national treasure
With his tawdry plays, the Rattigan of our days
I doubt, however much come out, he's no
Tennessee, as even blind Tiresias can see.
So much is chance as Goethe noted,
Missing Blackburn's turn as Gregory Fellow
Cost me a decade of dead ends
Thw lacklustre publicity of Redgrove and his ilk
A booming voice but poetry weak as water
Sixty before I fell into Hockney's pool
Of Proust and Mallarmė, Appolinaire and Reverdy.

Wystan, your iconic voice survived it all
Your Oxford American drawl enthralled my twenties
And the call of you, Hugh Mc Diarmid
Constructing the Lallans lingo while the masses
Flock to Corrie and to Bingo.

There were bright stars but few
Blackburn and Moraes to name but two,
Mostly the ghastly Armitage and his grosser lineage
I cannot name: they should construct
A statue to their shame.

Muse poets we must want and wait
The passing of this post-modern trash
Where Duffy and Jackie Kay still rule,
The naked empress and her royal fool.

A Surrealist Vision

There was a larger than life plastic cow
Tethered to a tree outside Hampstead Thameslink
Black and white bloated with full udders and a plot
Of imitation grass beneath her feet and
I wondered how she had arrived and why
A character from 'Cider with Rosie' had strayed
So far that particular wet Saturday and the effect
Was nothing short of miraculous and incongruous
Yet immensely attractive like Magritte's
Toy train emerging from a suburban hearth
And I was suddenly transported on a cloud
White with wonder to a field in what was once
England with scarecrows decked in overcoats
Their pockets stuffed with windfall apples
Who would break into speech and croak
"My name is Wurzel Gummidge" and I remembered
Puffins with their pastel covers at half a crown
And then the sky cleared and a wind blew
Small and keen and the dappled cow began to moo
As cows do and fifty years fell away and the train
Bore us through the darkening September night
The lights glowing in a mix of scarlet and pink
Like a Miro where cows graze on roof tiles and
Reverdy writes the script while Réda records it all
For me to translate and the railway company
Prints the poem on posters in violet ink
Always the favourite of René Crevelle
Mounted on every station platform
And the early stars twinkled and the full moon
Glowed and we were back in the cottage in Honley
Listening to milk churns loading and trains
Getting up steam and the night and the lights
Were one with the stars and the moon and the memories.

Intensive Care

for Brenda Williams

How long shall I stay?
Are there words to say?
The pain makes you mute,
Morphine has no song.
Forty- five years is a long
Time to be together and apart,
Husband and ex-husband, now
Carer for your cats who met
Me this morning bewildered
By your absence as I changed
And filled bowls and watched
Their bent heads lapping.

Sat by your bed, the drip,
The battery of instruments
Measuring input and output,
Flow charts, cannulas and clips,
The hands of the nurse move
With the precision of a pianist
From point to point, pressing,
Adjusting, constantly checking.
He waves the sister away when
His break is due, "I'll let you know
I've things to do."

I listen but your words are few
And drop to silence before
A sentence is half way through.
Your eyes close. I moisten
Your lips. The odds were against
But for a second time you survive
And when woke your question
"Are my cats alive?"

Two calls, twenty-two hours
Waiting for a diagnosis and you
At the point of death.
Three weeks on wards, IT3, IT4, DW7,
Numbers burned into my brain
With the memory of your pain,
The creases on your brow,
The steel clips, the ward rounds
I always missed, your terror
On discharge, your arms like sticks,
Your face swathed in death's pallor
You could just lift a cup,
The continuous nightmares,
The cats at the door,
The letters on the floor.

For weeks you waited
For me to come and count
The tablets, one by one,
Heat up food,
Feed the cats.
Slowly, how so slowly,
The cuts began to heal,
You moved more steadily,
The weeks passing,
A new month beginning.

February half through
You said you could get through
When my own op was due.
Nothing we were told
Was clinically true
The unmentionable pain,
The nightmares, the absolute
Lack of aftercare,
These we knew.
And so, like Lawrence, I may say,
"Look, we have come through"

Leaving Leeds

City of grief, city of dreams,
I am leaving you for the second time
For the last time, city of back-to-backs,
Kingdom of my heart, Kirkgate Market's
Domes and stalls, spiralling fruit and flowers,
Unable anymore to walk along your avenues
Of leather goods and gee-gaws bright as stars.

Sweet Aire sing softly while I spin my dreams
The deeper I dive into your Lethean streams
The higher I fly and like a hawk hunting I hurtle
Over cloudbanks hovering beyond the lost townships
Of Beeston and Armley, the mills gone with the trams
And throngs of my childhood companions,
How many, how many?

I have counted the bridges where I watched
The barges of my childhood glide, the streets where I played,
The ginnels tunnelled under sidings, hollows decked with flowers,
The silent bells of Crossgreen.

City of grief, city of dreams, I cannot laugh or cry
As you crumble and disappear like mercury on my palm
Between the cracks of memory, lines of disused tracks,
Brocaded banks of graves under arches,
Sweet Aire, sing softly while I spin my dreams.

Old Books

With sewn spines and dusty boards
Covers in cerise or saffron, backlists
Of poets, Roughton, Iremonger, Reed,
Thirties and forties pamphleteers
Who made it to Apocalypse anthologies
On war economy paper, print chafing
At font size confines, page limitations
And short runs relegated to dealers' basements
With spiders, soot and illustrated histories
Of World War One, naval almanacs
And thirties pacifist pamphlets, Gollancz
Left Book Club editions and the novels
Of Ethel M Dell.

Now the dealers have gone the way
Of all flesh, left as old flowers, lost hours
In the memories of attics and pavement
Boxes priced in shillings with pages missing
And names on corners, college bookplates,
Bede, Durham, Balliol in violet ink.

I secrete them in the loft up creaking ladders
With Dawson reprints of The Journal of Psychoanalysis
Titles tooled in silver on spines, tattered Folio editions
Of Proust, Hand and Flower Press Selecteds of Blackburn,
Grey Wall Tennysons, Poet & Printer Redgroves.
The gold of old books relegated to inaccessible places,
Corners of minds as odd as mine.

How long have we, or they?
Decades with luck but not that many
Between bouts of surgery, memorial services
As enemies, friends and vague acquaintances
Go into the ground or as smoke drift into
Cloud banks while early snowdrops huddle
In half-frozen new year soil.

The Fabulous Fifties

Fablon, formica and melamine
Those most lovely fabrics, first seen
When I was in my teens, green,
Yellow and orange of an aubergine
Unstainable, unbreakable and now unseen
Apart from in the windows of the retro shops
In Hampstead's South End Green, between
The sites where Jeremy Reed and Brenda Williams
Proceed to write for the most part unseen,
One a la Beauvoir in a café, the other on
The Pond Street protest green with me somewhere
Between, bridging these giants
Of the poetry scene.

23 May 2011

Ode on a Distant Prospect of The Hollows

Ring-fenced by eight feet high steel reinforced
Razor wired crash barriers,
Earthmovers, mechanical shovels and bulldozers
Shift mountains of soil and rubble
Making craters and mountains
From the landscape of my childhood.

There were streets there till the thirties
Then a fantasy playground for us all
Mounds of broken bricks, foxgloves,
Dandelions, cobbled roads leading to the
Land of Oz, runways and secret tracks,
Where our parents never ventured.

We had our last fire there, November fifth, 1954,
Obbo's dad climbed fifteen feet to light,
The guy tied to a chair.
I sat on a broken settee reading early Superman comics
Worth a fortune if only I'd known it.
Margaret Gardiner was with me, our last year
Together; we carried chumps from
Falmouth Terrace, star maps on our backs,
Eden if only we'd known it.

The Green Triangle

In Memory of Brian Haw

London's mafia monster Boris and Grinsta his fella gorilla
With Barrow from Westminster, Blair and Cameron
All dancing the conga, feeding children to Moloch,
Blake's tyger should trigger a seething volcano
Of civic disorder to free our green country
From Cameron the strangler, unjust Johnson,
Their placemen and planners, royalty's toadies,
Tourism's lackeys.
WE NEED A BURNING

Like the prophets of old Justice should descend
From the clouds and burn the Sodom and Gomorrah
Where a rodent-ridden traffic island, grubby, polluted,
Steel-fenced from freedom, shattered by sirens,
Accessible as Everest, targetted by every gung-ho politico
"For aesthetic reasons"- you've got to be joking
Its the fucking royal wedding with Sun readers waving
Their union jacks, tanked up on Tetleys, spitting and screaming,
Due process in hiding, justice abandoned to Johnson's gorillas
To Barrow from Westminster, the Royal Courts of Justice
Curtained in silence
When planning means banning
WE NEED A BURNING

Translations

Poems from the French

(2007)

Jacques Réda

January

What I love most about winter is the nakedness of branches
Against the pearl grey sky as daybreak mutes shadows
Into shades, blends them with pale smoke, stark against
The darkness. I imagine secretly staining the virgin horizon
With indelible ink, creating in secret a poem of the forest
That seems no more than a sepia snapshot, just one image remains,
The still branch without colour, writhing under the wind
Like a beggar's arm with grief its manifest. Between the dreaming
Depths of the void and the lowering wave of cloud forms
No hidden lesson or portent remains: only there
Where the air is occasionally crowded with hope or images.

Pierre Jean Jouve

Mozart

Your music is the rainbow
Of a mid-summer night's dream
Joy begins in your arias
Where oceans of despair
Are song birds taking wing.

A single columbine turns grass to meadow
So easily scythed away in summer
Nostalgia and tenderness, too,
Never go without pain
But have you seen
Salzburg's summer dawn
When clouds drink in the rising sun?

One day in those hills
And storm and rain are gone
O divine joy, soothe those suffering souls
Huddled in the world's dark concert halls.

Dream

Dream of your childhood sun
The one that shone when you were ten
How astonishing are the memories
When you concentrate as hard as you can
To see again the rose skies of heaven
How near, how real it remains
One colour, one rhythm, one desire.

She had such warmth
How easily she loved you
So passionate the memories
Running through the forest
Of long-gone dawns
Where in your heart
Those suns are ranged
Inviolable.

To have lived so
And been so loved
But now she is no more.

O that sun says now
How sad your childhood was.

from **'Nuptials' (1924)**

1

There's no need to be a king riding on a donkey
Everyone has his own conscience
We all wait; we travel endlessly
Without purpose.

We ourselves invented the machines of our own destruction
We should not complain of the outcome
As they smash everything in sight
Even the sun's rays fragment.

See how impotent I have become
How my anxieties have increased
How unstable I seem
I can barely hold myself together
I don't act my age
I'm all over the place.
My old trouble's back with a vengeance
Human blood's the one colour
Death is final whatever its guise
The walls are closing in
Nothing I can say alters reality
I dare do nothing more.

2

When I was young I loved time
But I couldn't bear to be the youngest in the family
How I loved the grass heavy with seed
The trees delighting in the sound
Of their own sighing branches.

When I was young I loved old things
Now I follow my shadow
As it tilts towards death
I've tasted time for too long
Perhaps with old age
Calm will come.

3

How many mistakes we make when we love so foolishly
In pursuit of some dubious ecstasy
The smell, the taste, the touch of a woman
Her suppleness
Her deceit
Her in whose soft pearly skin
Smiles death itself who knows so well
The grief love ends in.

To My Lady

Incurable passion! Incurable wound
Unquenchable red leaves burn in the shadows
Your once fair hair darkens
Mocks the naked demons of my desire

Your smile has become a grimace
As my bloody wounds gape
Your bitter smile flits by
Your eyes glow like stone
Your hair ornaments my grave
Your mask is a close-up of death

You parade folly as wisdom
Inscribing my name on your tomb

Stephane Mallarmé

The Apparition

A melancholy moon where dreaming angels wept
Pale tears aid the beam the hazy flowers kept
And fingering their bows drew from a thousand strings
A symphony of clouds to gild an angel's wings.

The memory of the kiss you gave
Wove sadness through my dreams and days,
Held for a moment in the mind
Made human passion but a blind.
I searched the pavements of the night
But you came dancing in the sun
And scattered from half-opened hands
The perfumed tears the stars begun.

André Hardellett

The Dance of Night

The muses of Bercy Pier
Took me as far as Grenelle
And their sisters of Grange-aux-Belles
Dropped me by the winter gardens of Passy
Night and the muses of Bercy
Have reached an understanding.

I'd often travel round Paris, harbour of dreams
Forever open to night's wanderers
And their lifetime friends
Journeying through dusk
To disappear at break of day
I'd often travel round Paris, harbour of dreams.
Restif, Nerval, Apollinaire,
Leon Paul Fargue and all that crew
Those who showed me a way through
Will light all my to-morrows
And point the road to the isles of dawn
Restif, Nerval, Apollinaire…

Sundays in my heart
Start from Paris-Bastille
Rush to the eldorados of Marne
With the blonde in the low cut dress
Her breasts already decked with jonquils
Sundays in my heart…

Greetings, dancers in the back streets!
Bastille day is here at last
Girls enough for a bouquet
Of summer heat waves drifting past
Inviting us to back street banquets
Greetings, dancers everywhere!

The sound of music fades
In an accordion's sigh
Already shadows caress the street
Where neon signs are rushing by
In amber magic DANCE
The sound of music fades.

I came and could not find you
Absence for only a single night sorely grieves me
O Venetian girl who so aroused me
With your blonde hair in my dreams
I'd recognise you anywhere
But came to find you gone

Night outside whispers in my ear
As I watch its petals fall
On all the hidden happiness of all
Fusing in the release of a girl's first orgasm
Outside night whispers in my ear.
We came together the very second
Everest's pinnace dazzled
All the lovers of the world combined!
Some died while others reached the summit
Together at that very second…
Much later - when the day was breaking -
I found myself at La Villette
With broad- girthed waiters, aprons
Spotted with blood, tearing bread,
The milkman late and day about to break.

Alone, his eyes fixed on his glass,
A taciturn waiter leans on the counter:
He is a brother to me
I recognise his despair
His hours of regret,
Alone his eyes fixed on his glass.

O you, our lifetime friends,
As dawn inexorably comes
You disappear into the shadows
As the clock strikes eight I beg you,
Pray for us and those we love,
O you, our lifetime friends.

Jaques Prévert

Barbara

Do you remember, Barbara,
That night it was raining over Leeds
And we were walking together
You were smiling, laughing, ecstatic
In spite of the rain
Remember, Barbara it was raining
Over Leeds, endlessly raining
When I met you in Street Lane
You were smiling and I was, too,
You, who I hardly knew,
Remember, remember that night all the same.

There was the shadow of another
And he shouted your name, Barbara,
Briefly you embraced him but I knew
You were still mine, dripping, happy
And blooming in the rain
Remember that and don't be annoyed with me
If I try to get close to you again
Like love and the rain I cannot change.

Never forget how that wise and happy rain
Fell on your smiling face and made
All Leeds smile, that rain on the moored barge,
On the Aire and Roundhay Park Lake.
O, Barbara, what a sad mess life is!
What happened to you beneath the iron rain,
Beneath the rain of fire, steel and blood?
The shadow of another who pressed himself
Lovingly against you, perhaps it is beginning to fade.

Oh, Barbara, it is raining endlessly over Leeds
Just as it did on the night we met
It is still not quite the same
But your voice has grown soft again.

Paul Eluard

1945 – Year of Peace

I have passed through winter's gates
Through the portals of bitterness
For a single kiss

O city scaled down
To the size of my rented room
Where evil gathers its harvest of stars

O year of peace I have only you
For mentor; to be truly human I must learn
To stop looking in the mirror

Dawn

The sun runs riot across the world entire-
I am as much a part of it as I am of you-
The sun enslaves the whole wide world
And lights beneath a night of stars
The smiles of those who dream of dawn.

Pleasure's whole mystery-
A battle of bewilderments
The lot of all who dwell
Beneath the sun
Turns each against the other
Each against his brother.
O you I now consign to memory
Who was my earth, my sun, my mystery.

Perhaps

You could do no other than gather
The hearts cut into the tree bark
Smiles and laughter, softness beyond knowing,
Conqueror or conquered, you shine like an angel
High in the sky, in the very tree tops.

Far above a battle-weary muse whimpers,
Falls to the foot of the hill.

However Sad those See-through Clouds

You cannot help but fall in love

Days pass beyond counting, flowers wither,
Seeds gone forever.

At the end of the white wilderness
Only dog days remain.

Before the Eyes of a Dead Pauper

A colour-wash of shells
Music of bare white arms
Birds and wind are one.

O.V.De L.milosz

Autumn Song

Listen to the night wind's voice
Ominous and cracked with age
Both harbinger of death and soother of the newly born
Listen to the wind's voice.

All your griefs, my sad one, are in vain,
Implacable forgetfulness falls
On friends' and lovers' graves
Listen to the wind's voice.

She is with you, if only for a moment,
Playing the sonatas of long gone days and nights
Forget her, she is gone so far, so very far away
Listen to the wind's voice.

To-morrow we shall dream of the remains of the day
We must prepare our last good-byes
Whether we mean them, yea or nay,
Listen to the voice of the wind.

Gerard De Nerval

Delficia

Daphne, my old flame, do you remember the spot
At the sycamore's foot, under the laurels pale,
Beneath the olives, myrtles and the listless reeds,
Inspirer of my tremulous first song?

Do you remember the temple's peristyle,
The taste of bitter lemons on your tongue,
The grotto where the imprudent ones woke
Dragons slumbering since time began?

They will return, those gods and ghosts you mourn,
However drear and deep the Sibyll's cell
She will be loosed to cry and call
That livid wish not to be born at all.

Pierre Reverdy

Transparencies of Day

The cloud-formed sails
The birds' wings outspread
A passing voice
Deserted borders
Always watched

The vastness of all creation
The air vibrates with memory
The wing beats ebb
The lonely cries are stacked
The forced march of invaders along our shores

Higher than the tree
Further than Christ's fingertips
Stretched on the Cross
Dishevelled shadows
And on the open road
Daybreak without end

Breath of the West Wind

Words scattered to the wind
    The pearls of a necklace
    And the hand beneath the glove
The star tremble of nightfall
    A single eye a watching passer-by
    I don't know a soul
    As night falls
    Shadows mock me.

Behind I sense fear
Pressing everywhere
The speeding car
The endless stretch of water
The faces in the waves
The hands
Nothing
Not even a shadow
The pupil of a single distant eye watches
The mysterious white body
A car crosses the night's stillness
No word is spoken
A faint noise in the air
The sails of a windmill stir

Gold Water

The stream is flecked
With gold specks of light
Spinning circles of warmth
And the heart abruptly stops
While the bridge grasps still higher
Nearer the sleepy old coach-house
Its frontage swilled with spills of light
    Where the silence is set
        In fitting symbols
    And wounded brows
Afternoon has closed the gate
Echo mounts guard over the approaching foot-falls
The currents of cold air suffocate in the shadows
    In the trees heavy with dew
        On the dusty slopes
    Broad as a river in spate
Cloud forms cross the spumes of seafoam
        And the tilled fields' furrows
The weighed-down cart and the wingless plane
        The corpses's dead weight
And the gathered voices of night
        The veils of reality
And the blue havens
        The stars of harbour lights.

Naming Wings

The same bird who built his nest
Between the ladder and the tree
    The clock was chiming
The voices trapped between the windows
Side by side with pocket watches on gold chains
    Striking mid-day.

And the sounds of the streams rise to the rooftops
    Between both pathways
    Caught in the headlights
    Vibrant motes of light
    And it is dusk already
He is the one who stops by the billboard
    To ask directions
    Over the rooftops of the town
    To the Orient or to the sea's calm

A door in the clouds opens
On a darkness more profound
Than the backdrop to the stars
Where a single star twinkles
A nameless craft under sail.

The Sounds of Evening

From the thorns of a burning bush
The chimney spews
Great gob-fuls
Over the distant sky
The shades of night
Blurred indistinct
Fall over the rock's shards
Where the wind warps the way
The air is grey
In the direction of naked open arms
Time will return soon enough
The harsh outline of the low monastery walls
The space from the trees
To the gap where the bridge is raised
Where the road lies straight as a die
Dates scribbled on the wall
And scattered cries
All that passes over yonder
In these worthless times
And it is I
Stood at the parapet's edge
My face against the iron grille
Under time's dry dust
A whiter shade of pale
When the questioner is framed against the light
When distant bells toll
And the one I call to
Answers the lonely echo
In a changed voice
Speaking my name in a way
I no longer recognise as my own
A pale silhouette
Wrinkles crossing my brow
The reflections of a shadow.

Thorn

What use is the orb of this uncertain world?
Hidden, turned back,
What use is night
With its cruel face
The great mystery where nothing changes
Whatever I reach out and touch-still nothing,
Thought sculpted in unveined marble
Blue threads of water cool my soul's ardours
The sun keeps on these disenchanted days.
Light without shadow over grey marshland
Until our bones, too, turn into the ribs of roads
The fine grey powder limbs ground down to
Light's rays illumine.
Hazard of fortune
Hazard of hands
Movements in the cold of morning
When every leaf in my garden
Shatters in the wind like glass
Arid under a wilting shadow
My heart beats by yours.

Turning Road

There is a terrible grey in the weather
Great gusts of wind from the south
Hardly audible lappings of water
Capsize the evening vivid with
The plaintive tone of alien voices.

The taste of ash on my tongue
Mingles with the sound of an organ
Eyes are moist like blades of grass
When barefoot dew touches leaves
At hardly day-break.
Someone searches for lost address
Down a hidden road of far-stretched stars
Far-flung flowers where a lost stream
Wipes its careless lips.

When the pilgrim's footsteps cross
The sundial counting rhythms and
Painting horizons all the shouting
Has died away and the weather
Meets itself coming back.

As for me I'm of to heaven
Eyes stuck to sunbeams a pointless hubbub
In my head where livid faces hover
All that has passed away this holiday
All my uncounted days.

Grief's Destiny

I wonder at the open door in the white wall
At the roof and the field's slope behind the house
A hand holds the earth entire between its fingers
As the stippled spear of sky catches the hare's red fur
While nature flees west and leaves me to watch
The sky's impassable roads.

In winter rain I hear the SOS from sinking ships
The caterwaul of castaways yet we are still
So far from the sea itself
A chain of hills surrounds the hollows
Of the rigging's last lights.

Words traced on trees slowly open boats
Skim waves before the lighthouse
With its warning beam.

A blind bird's song gathers me in in
Token of the wind's words
As to the lie of the land
The least threat
Keeps it from taking off.

The rainbow's glimmer
Crosses this sinister abandoned land
Until it is gone.

If everything I've seen
Proves me wrong only this full sail
Makes me safe in what I have and hold
Letting the slope's last light
Some sad gesture
A bitter glance
At what might have been

Robert Desnos

I Have Dreamed of You So Much

I have dreamed so much of you that you are no longer real
Have I still enough time left reach out and touch your living body
And to kiss with my lips the source of the voice
That is so dear to me?

I have dreamed of you so much that my arms,
Used to being crossed upon my breast while clasping your shadow
Would perhaps not bend themselves to your body's outline.

Faced with the reality of what has haunted and daunted me
For days and years inevitably I would become a shadow.
What justice does life hold?

I have dreamed of you so much that there is no time left
For me to wake up. I sleep standing
My body exposed to all the appearance of love and life
And you, the only woman who could be for me today
With your red lips and smooth brow and lissom body.
I have dreamed of you so much, walked with your image,
Spoken to your ghost, slept with your shadow,
That nothing is left for me except to be a phantom
And a hundred times more of a shadow
Among phantoms than the shadow
Which moves so cheerfully over the sundial of your life.

No, love is not dead in this heart of mine
Nor in my eyes or mouth, whatever reality
Says to the contrary.

Listen, I've had my fill of the picturesque
And of colours and charm; I love love
With all its tenderness and cruelty.
My love has only your name

All else goes by, whatever other mouths
Have pressed themselves against mine
My love has only one name, one form and it is yours.

If some day you remember it, whose image and name
You bear, one day on the road between Leeds and London,
At dusk when the sun's last beams are reflected
On the Aire's dark waters or else on
A night of storms, of infinite stars
Or on the bonnet of a fast car on a spring day
On the M1 or on a rainy day or at dawn
I tell your spirit that I was the one who loved you most
And that it is a pity you never knew it.

Say to yourself that we must not regret things
Ronsard and Baudelaire before me have sung
The regrets of long dead women who scorned the purest love.

When you are dead you will still be beautiful and desirable
And I shall be already dead, enclosed completely
In your immortal body, in your astonishing image
Ever present among the perpetual wonders of life and eternity.

But if I live your voice with its softness,
Your glance with its warmth,
The smell of your hair on the nape of your neck
And every secret part of your body
Will live in my memory, in me who am only myself
And neither Ronsard nor Baudelaire
But because I have known you and loved you
I am their equal.

I am myself in order to love you
And wish for no other fame than that
And for no other reputation
In this despicable world.

Pierre Emmanuel

In The Shadows

When the music of my eyes finally fades
And my spirit's shadow crosses Lethe
My hands helpless, my head cradled in the stars
Where the forgotten heavens are my harbour
When life's bitter weariness has abandoned the body
After a lifetime of borrowings, infidelity and desire,
Unfeeling and reckless lurches towards the absurd
Against the vertigo of fathomless grief
My spirit moves in death's orbit
In a world etched in spirit
By a nothingness that cannot be stayed.

Sadly the illustrious weariness of being me
A contraption of limited perception and sumptuous ennuie
And the beckonings of heaven - all will disappear
At a single stroke of the emptiness which covers everything,
Fills the void and sustains my spirit.
In absence everything is clear
In the purity of form nonbeing gives to nakedness
There and there alone may God be seen.

The world I was so greedy to possess
Without a breath of wind or single tree-
God bears the weight of all the grieving dead
With their unyielding tears and furrowed brows-
Never, never, o mute and awesome world,
Will I again be part of you, for I am dead.

Yet I will hear again the music of vision
In a world beyond the given
Veiled in a breaking dawn
Where clouds are woven by unseen hands
The plainsong of newly born stars awakens me
With cloud forms of an unending sea.

André Frenaud

The Old Country

Myths and stories are formed beneath our very feet
But already nostalgia clouds their glories
Our country is coming apart; do go and make away
With what remains so we may have another Eden.

I have delayed overlong to do justice
I can delay no longer, man of the future,
I must get to know you in my dreams.
O what visions have delighted our eyes
What joys our hands have touched.

O first world, you are still with us,
How I love those who hear its sounds,
Who know how to listen, having kept open
The tentative ears of childhood,
They alone will inherit the spirit
Borne on the wings of stars.

They go forward, carried along by the voices they encounter,
They will stay at the fair until the last lights die
The kindness they meet at every turn
Will never lead them astray
They find a woman dreaming, drawing water at the well,
A family serving soup with leeks and bread,
Altars set up on mountain slopes.
The man who made the pact of old
Stands still, late and full of remorse.

In Memoriam

Brenda Williams
10th December 1948 – 19th July 2015

Only music can stem the blood wrench of my heart
Your death began but nine weeks on
Every day your absence wakes me at four a.m.
I can never tell you how much I miss you
Words flowed between us like a river

Cut Flowers

for Brenda Williams

I remember the bungalow at Rawdon
Where we met, burning coals could never warm it,
Living there alone was like wearing a hair shirt.
I had reached the end of childhood, the part
With jelly, ludo and Rupert Bear. You came
With a friend who announced, 'There's no one here
Who's not neurotic'.

I had paid half a crown to have the grass clipped
And someone had brought a Procul Harum lp,
'A Whiter Shade of Pale' was our lullaby
But the night ended with nothing said.
Failure dogged us wherever we went,
The Wordsworthian cottage at Hall Ings, the turkey farm
At Hoylehouse, the semi in Oakes. Parenthood
Is best forgotten, Isaiah seemed never to sleep,
Neighbours became strangers so we left for Leeds
And subsisted while you wrote your first poems
To the sound of Beethoven's Late Quartets.

Decades of war with truces and battles neither
Won nor lost, now you are sixty-six with cancer
And a future measured in months. I am seventy three
With a bad knee and even my optimism
Is starting to fray.
There are pictures on my wall, one has you
At your protest against bed cuts, stood beside
A placarded poem, one is of me with a kitten of yours
And the third is Haworth, heather moors
And moving clouds.

There is no campaign I can fight, no letters
To write. Days have to be counted, appointments made,
Taxis booked. The day a year ago when
You were diagnosed I said, 'You're dying'
And you are still but more quickly and forty seven years
Of mutual living are giving way like a bridge of planks.
My foxes howl in the alley and at the stall
The girl cuts flowers and words are stones.

4th January 2015

Your Dying

How can I endure winter without you, sad divine daughter
Of September? Your calls outlast autumn's miasma,
The hesitant tone of your final poem 'Towards an Obituary',
Self-questioning, plaintive Keatsian ardour, harbour
Of all your griefs, your mother's slow death from cancer,
Denied the fare for her last hospitalisation.

When they said you were terminal, "Three or four months
And a bit" You tried hard to finish 'The Poet',
'Brian's Not There', 'Forever Young'. It was hopeless,
So you fled to the South Bank to watch the films
You'd missed, a season of Siodmak,
Welles in 'Chimes at Midnight'.

You managed a whole Saturday, Hardy's
'Under the Greenwood Tree' in three two hour episodes
But the next day you phoned at seven,
"Please get me into hospital".

It was the last time, after twelve days they moved you
To the hospice. I sat in the transfer ambulance,
You were strapped down and I strapped up, too far
To grasp your desperate hand. For once your terror was plain,
You'd never come home to your eight cats again.

I was the only visitor to the hospice, save Daisy
To assure your cradle Catholic soul of a Christian burial.
In those last twelve days you awaited death while I,
Hopeless and stunned, listened for your last breath.

Brenda Williams Nhs Protester Extraordinaire

(*Born Leeds 1948 - Died London 2015*)

We are the words, we are the music
—Virginia Woolf

The threat of closing the West Hampstead Day Hospital,
Art therapy nine to five, your home for a decade,
Left you inconsolable and incandescent.
You had eighty-four placards printed,
Pushing them every day up the hill,
Tying them to railings the length of Hampstead Green,
'Save our NHS' to 'The Great and the Good
Of Hampstead ,Where are you?'
Under the baleful glare of Andrew Way, the C.E.,
Who hated you from day one and plotted
With Camden Council to have you gone.

You didn't win, they closed Fordwych Road
And threw in a hundred acute beds.
The patients kept their distance, every one,
But for two years you kept on, ignoring the looks
Of loathing, the spitting, the plotting.
Three times they came for you, the police
Held you while the council inspectors
Tore the placards down, one by one.

The sheer weight of the hatred, the ignorance
Of what you were doing, inspired you
To write 'Lament for the Day Hospital'
In fourteen scorching sonnets and moved you
To St Pancras to protest the death of Margaret Walsh,
Godmother to Damien Hirst, 'Left at the door of a
Closed ward' to die by her own hand.

Way at the Free went back to Australia;
There were questions about 'appointing
                    unqualified friends'
He felt unable to answer and Coroner Reid
Was dismissed for something similar.

How do I fill the void you left?
The sound of your tread on the path
Your phone line cut off.

Journey Into The Next Room

i.m. Brenda Williams 1948–2015

Il ne faut pas aller plus loin
Les bijoux sont pris dans la lyre
Les pappillons nous du dilire
Remuent sans y penser la cendre du couchant

You don't have to go far
The jewels are frozen in the lyre
The black butterflies of delirium
Unthinking stir the sleeper's fire
Pierre Reverdy *Le Coeur Tournant*

I thought to find within the very rooms of life
That other room whose door you'll open
Yet still be as I have always known you.
I've tried to find some beaten track
Where words may be hand-sewn sails
And fingers grasp the tiller to steer
A last sad ship, ease it out of harbour
Onto a sea bereft, fathom this journey
From celestial charts to the far havens
In an age which has snatched away
The key to the chest
Where charts lie heavy with dust,
The secret only you will hold
The entry to which I cannot pass
Nor know the passage to or through
No matter how hard I look, how long I search
Crevices in walls, cracks in boards,
Scarlet, yellow or white blooms
Spring through a strange season.

These lines I thought would come
On a dark day or yet more darker night
Already are the furrows, the very sea lanes
Where you alone will steer, your own hands

Fashioned over years, the barque whose creaking masts
You heard before the sails were set,
Your nimble fingers tugged to pull
The thread through all the canvas sheets
Gathered in that very room I sought in vain.

The time in which we live and die is one
Where death itself has ceased to be,
Are passing years, the rowing after God
On rivers that have ceased to run,
Water courses long gone, charts smudged
Beyond recall, signs rusted and unread,
Unfathomed depths, unpeopled shores whose breath
Has blown across the glass
Where the shadow of our glance remains.

These eighteen months this journey planned
By other hands has waxed and waned
Along the shores, contours of a map
No weather vane can point to,
Neither west nor east, no legend
Measuring miles, no compass,
Or map to lands that none holds title to,
No building, no being-in-itself, no being
Yet at all, yet not nothing either in our age
Of surfaces where show is all,
The hand that writes in sign or symbol,
Cuneiform or Rosetta Stone.

Beyond the vision of the cataracts which dim
Our sight or make it over to a symphony
Where notes fade into silence or rise, then
Fade again upon a seamless shore.
For fifty years you have awaited death
As some relief from grief etched in your very soul,
Your eyes always on a blind horizon fixed.

A journey you alone can make
It is beyond me even in sand
And with a stick to point a map or contour
Or seize upon a colour
For a chart that skies unknown will look upon
In brightest day or darkest night, yet not
An end or a beginning but more a kind
Of quite another time, a spirit realm,
A crystal cave of making, a place where words fail,
Where language is not words, where pictures
Are, as Rothko said, a merge of colour,
Bars of vermilion shading into yellow,
Blue into magenta, Turner's *Fighting Temeraire.*

These words so mortal tear and break
Like hands scrabbling on sheer rock wall
Or uttered once have no echo or my tongue is mute
My ears can hear no sound at all
The midnight of my life, such as it has
So reluctantly become, a rowing desperately to God
When God has ceased to be
Where hope was never there at all
But only faith beating on a shore
Turning on a wave has meaning any more
And light from darkness comes
If only I can find that door.

5th June 2015

Epilogue

Waking suddenly I searched for Reverdy and Baudelaire and having dipped briefly into their sweet bitterness I solaced myself with swallowing a lozenge of honey and memory I keep by my side for such awakenings. It was you Jeannie and Ali too, a meeting in a pub after half a century of separation and we were laughing and taking turns to sample smiles left by a passing angel. We mingled with a crowd losing and refinding each other and every encounter began with a caress and yes we all had loyalties to other loves but after all it was a dream and the summation was when we set to clear a mountain of washing-up, chasing plates with buckets of foam, bubbles falling and floating, mingling with a forever of hugs and smiles strewn on a hazed grass bank which made us all slightly drunk as we rummaged for lost threads. There were no memories as time had never happened and the slight change to our appearance was put down to forgetfulness and the refound affection in rainbows children reach to in a neutral sky and we sighed as the dream was put by and held each other before the lid was sealed by an angel in exile.

About the Author

Barry Tebb was born in Leeds in 1942. He studied English at Leeds Training College and sat at the feet of a series of Gregory Fellows in Poetry at the University of Leeds including Martin Bell, Peter Redgrove, Jon Silkin and David Wright. His first collection, *The Quarrel with Ourselves,* was praised by John Carey in *The New Statesman* and he appeared in *Three Regional Voices* alongside Michael Longley and Ian Crichton-Smith. He edited *Five Quiet Shouters* which included work by the then unknown Angela Carter. In 1995 he founded Sixties Press and has edited the magazines, *Leeds Poetry Weekly* and *Poetry Leeds.*

His first novel *Pitfall Street* in 2004, as was his *Sixties Press Anthology of Gregory Fellows in Poetry* (with Dr. Debjani Chatterjee) and *Tranquillity Street: New and Selected Poems.*

Barry Tebb has written, edited and published over thirty books and pamphlets. He worked with the poet and protester Brenda Williams campaigning for better mental health facilities nationwide until her death from cancer in July 2015. Tebb was included in Michael Horovitz ground-breaking Penguin Anthology *Children of Albion* (1969) and edited *Orphans of Albion* (2008)